SECRETS,
SINS, STRUGGLES, STRESS, SURVIVING

A Woman's Transformation From Pastors' Mistress to the Pulpit

Dr. Gloria Milow

SECRETS,
SINS, STRUGGLES, STRESS, SURVIVING

A Woman's Transformation From
Pastors' Mistress to the Pulpit

Dr. Gloria Milow

MILLIGAN BOOKS   CALIFORNIA

Copyright © 2005 by Dr. Gloria Milow
Los Angeles, California

Printed and Bound in the United States of America

Published and Distributed by:
Milligan Books, Inc.

Cover Layout by
Interior Design by Milligan Books

First Printing, April 2005

ISBN: 0-9767678-0-5

All Rights Reserved

Milligan Books
1425 West Manchester Boulevard, Suite C
Los Angeles, CA 90047
www.milliganbooks.com
drrosie@aol.com
(323) 750-3592

All rights reserved. No part of this book may be reproduced in whole or in part, in any form or by any means, electronic or mechanical, including photocopying, recording or by any information storage and retrieval system, without permission in writing from the author.

Dedication
This Book is Dedicated to:

My Mother and late Stepfather
Mrs. Elease E. Nelson & Isaac Nelson

My Father and Stepmother
Mr. Sululah Milow & Annie Mae Milow

My Children
Phamesha L. Johnson, the late James Russell
Johnson Jr., Michael G. Johnson,
and Elease Milow Simmons

My Grandchildren
Jaylin Michael Johnson and
Sydney Lelani Sonnier Johnson

My Brothers
The late Sululah Milow Jr. & Adrian K. Milow

My Grandmothers
The late Martha Greene (Mo-Mo) &
the late Bessie Milo (Ma Bessie)

My Great-Great-Aunt
The late Ella Nevilles Fisher

To My Children

I know you have criticized me, and that's okay,

I've done my best.

I have given you love, punished you, and spanked you,

Everything I could give you I did, except my life.

Jesus did that. He paid it all and **all** to Him I owe.

I did what I knew best. This thing called parenting is a daily job (on the job training).

Kids, believe me, in all my ups and downs with you, God had my back.

I never meant to hurt you, mistreat you, or desert you in any way.

I never abandoned any of you. God helped me fight our battles.

If you feel that I did hurt you in any way, please know that I am not perfect.

Please forgive me in Jesus' name.

Again, I love all of you so very much.

To My Grandchildren

Even though your mothers deny me the privilege of seeing you and will not allow you to visit me, I still love both of you so very much.

Table of Contents

Dedication 5
Acknowledgments 9
About the Author 11
Preface 13
Introduction 21
Chapter 1: My Sad, Fast Exit from Louisiana 23
Chapter 2: Life in Southern California 29
Chapter 3: Seduction. 37
Chapter 4: My School Life 43
Chapter 5: My First Marriage 47
Chapter 6: My First Teaching Assignment 53
Chapter 7: My First Child 57
Chapter 8: The Birth of James Jr. 61
Chapter 9: Separation 65
Chapter 10: June–June's Life and Illness 71
Chapter 11: Final Separation. 85
Chapter 12: Lil Girl Growing Up wth Nana Ella 91
Chapter 13: Stress and Death 95
Chapter 14: Marriages Not Ordained by God 105
Chapter 15: Violent Attack 109
Chapter 16: Deep Throat 111
Chapter 17: The Pulpit 115
Chapter 18: Golden Birthday Year 2002 119
Chapter 19: The Terrible Night! 127
Chapter 20: My Prayer for My Son 133

Chapter 21: Home Going Celebration—I Eugolized
   My Son..135
Chapter 22: Face It, It's for Real.....................143
Chapter 23: Stepping Out in Faith..................151
Chapter 24: Conclusion............................153

Acknowledgments

TO GOD BE THE GLORY! Thank you, God, for keeping my mind. So many times I didn't think I could make it. *"With God, all things are possible to him who believes."*

To my mother, Elease Nelson—Your strength I indeed admire. You have experienced the death of your mother, your son, your husband, and now your oldest grandson, your 'June Boy.' In all that you have gone through, you have fostered eight more children at your ripe and wonderful age. Thank you, Mom, for your love, your prayers, and for your spiritual, emotional, and financial support.

To my daughter Phamesha—Thank you for helping me stay focused.

To my daughter Little Elease—Thanks for understanding me while I was writing.

To my darling son, Michael—Thank you for your hugs, kisses, and most of all, for your input into my book!

To Yolanda Adams—Thank you for your beautiful song, "The Battle's Not Yours—It's The Lord's." I listened to this song over and over again day and night.

To Dr. Milligan—Thank you for all of your help, love, and kindness, and for helping me get through such an awesome task. Thanks for making my dream a reality.

To Beatrice Cunningham-Davis (author of *I Cry No More*)—Thanks for coming to see me and sharing your story of the loss of your beloved son, Andre.

To Dr. Cranford Scott—Thanks for being my wonderful doctor.

To William Bill Cosby—For sharing your loss of your son.

To Bishop TD Jakes (author of *Woman, Thou Art Loosed*)—Thanks for the seminars. Now I **am** loosed from my bondages (bondages that **NO** woman has ever discussed openly).

For all of my friends who helped me in numerous ways, there are too many names to list—you know who you are, Thank You.

About the Author

DR. GLORIA MILOW IS THe founder and pastor of MG's Full Gospel Church. She has thirty years of experience in teaching and counseling, and has been an assistant principal. She holds three lifetime credentials in California in the following areas: Pupil Personnel (counseling) (k-12); English, Psychology, Sociology (7-12); and Psychology (Community College) and an education leadership (k-12) in Georgia. Gloria is a native of New Orleans, Louisiana. She is an entrepreneur & previous owner of "Classie Fashions by Marie." She has owned multiple businesses in Los Angeles and was the owner of Milow's Family Child Care.

Dr. Milow received her AA degree in General Studies from Compton College in Compton, California, February 1972; a BS degree in Sociology, Psychology, and English from Pepperdine University in Los Angeles, August 1972; a MA degree in Educational Psychology from Azusa Pacific with honors, May 1978; and her Ph.D. in Pastoral Ministry from Eternal Word Graduate School in Carson, California, with a 4.0 grade point average, October 2001.

Gloria is the mother of four children, Phamesha, the late James Jr., Michael Johnson, and Elease Milow-Simmons. She fostered three groups of children, a total of eight, for four years. The judge even gave her permission to take them out of state on vacation.

Gloria always knew that she was destined for greatness despite her many struggles with sin and stress. She was locked in bondage because of secrets, but survived. At the tender age of seventeen, she became the mistress for several very prominent pastors in Los Angeles and New Orleans, Louisiana; in fact, she became the madam for these pastors.

Dr. Milow suffered five failed marriages. Then on July 26, 2002, she suffered a crushing blow when her son, James Russell Johnson Jr., was murdered in cold blood while talking on his cellular phone only two blocks from his home.

Approximately 7 P.M.—the same hour that her son was murdered—Dr. Milow was at her church having all night prayer service. She was praying to God, asking Him to save her children and cover them with His precious blood.

Pastor Milow has performed the eulogy for many young men, and now she had to eulogize her elder son. Her comfort is found in the Holy Word. During this painful period, she also gathered strength from a song by Yolanda Adams entitled, "The Battle is not yours, it's the Lord's."

These five Ss have been a part of Dr. Milow's life—A Secret I've kept, I Sinned, I Struggled, I was Stressed, but yet, I've Survived—all in Jesus' name. Not only has she survived, she has OVERCOME!

Preface

SOMETIMES PEOPLE FEEL THAT THEY were born with bad luck, or that they were dealt a bad hand. Some might even think that God must have forgotten about them, or that He is punishing them for something they've done, or for something their fathers did—the sins from previous generations being revisited upon them.

Some ask the question, where is God when things go wrong? I want you to ask yourself the question, where was *I* when things went wrong? Can you imagine what it must be like for a pastor/minister who is preaching, teaching, and standing on the Word to lose a child by means of a violent crime? We must understand that God does not have our children killed; that is the work of Satan.

God is faithful to His promises to you. He said that He would never leave you nor forsake you, and that He will comfort you—and He will! Satan is faithful, too. His job is to steal, kill, and destroy; and that's what he does. Satan does not discriminate when it comes to his works. He seeks to destroy all.

If we would fine-tune our ears to hear and to distinguish the voice of God from the voice of Satan, we would avoid many pitfalls in life. People often say, "Something told me this or that." Well, you had better recognize *who* that something is—He is the Holy Spirit.

This fine-tuning of the spiritual ear comes via studying God's Word, meditation, praise, and having a prayer life.

The Holy Spirit will lead us if we will follow. It is when we are driven by our egos and our fleshly desires that we miss the voice of God. When status and material things of this kingdom drive us, we can easily miss His voice.

God wants us to have good marriages. He values family. It is not His will that we have broken or failed marriages. The problem is that we are not in tune with our spiritual ear to seek God's approval for our potential mate. We marry for too many reasons other than for the *right* reason.

Today, I listen to God. In 2003, God told me to uproot from California and to move to Georgia. I did just that. I left my family behind. I can truly tell you my faith is in God, and my desire is to please Him. "*Without faith, it is impossible to please Him.*" When God gives us a vision, He doesn't give it to anyone else in the family. Your family and friends will not hear His voice; therefore, you cannot count on them for advice or confirmation.

I am in no way trying to preach to you. I am making my life an open book, that you may see the kind of mess that God can clean up. The great TD Jakes is making sure women are loosed from bondages. However, I have never heard of any woman being loosed from the bondage of being a madam, or mistress, **to her pastor**. There may be others out there right now. Maybe you are still enjoying the life. I had to be loosed of this secret bondage. I was not the only female member serving these pastors. Many times I rode on the same elevator with women from my congregation as we went to or came from the den of pastoral iniquity.

What I am about to tell you next is very hard for me to say because I am a preacher. Please do not misunderstand me. I want to make it crystal clear that there are more good, godly pastors than there are bad, ungodly pastors. I urge young teens and young adult women to seek counseling from their own parents or from some of the elderly women in the church if this passage speaks to you about your situation. Many pastors use their power and their members' money to abuse and to take advantage of needy, trusting, and naïve women.

Women are the predominate members of our congregations. Are we really there for the message or the messenger? Many years ago, I sat in churches, watching preachers whop and holler and saw women jumping, shouting, and passing out. Why? I am not the one to judge the Holy Ghost (Holy Spirit), but clearly, I know what I saw. I have a much better understanding of these things now.

Some Common Sayings I have heard so-called ministers claim to be biblical. These sayings are not scripture –sayings such as:

- A bird in hand is worth two in the bush
- Love is blind
- Heartfelt religion
- What is to be will be
- Time and tide wait for no man
- Every tub must sit on its own bottom
- Beggars should not be choosey
- Think twice before you speak
- All is well, that ends well
- Procrastination is the thief of time
- Everything that glitters ain't gold
- I'm gonna put on my long white robe and walk the pearly gates

Please study the Bible for yourself.
I am healed of my scars and wounds. It is not my intent to hurt or cause pain for anyone; therefore, I will not provide names of the pastors or other men who used my

madam clientele. I can tell you that these were pastors of large congregations in Los Angeles, California, and New Orleans, Louisiana. I pray that they have changed. Now I see that drug heads, drunks, alcoholics, people involved in nightclubbing, prostitution, and pimping ain't no worse than some pastors living secret lives of shame.

I know better now, and I know who I am and from where my resources come—God Almighty.

As I mentioned in my autobiography, I have had five failed marriages. I believe that my teen years—being the preacher's mistress—impacted my relationships with other men. I learned how to be unfaithful. The Bible teaches that "*You reap what you sow.*" At the age of 17, my pastor would send a limousine to my house to bring me to him at a hotel. He would invite his pastor friends to our room. He said to his friends that if he found out that I was with them in his absence, that he would kill them.

Once I did secretly meet with another pastor. He wanted more from me than what his money could pay for. He begged me not to tell the other pastor for fear of his life. I did not tell, because I believed he would have been killed. Sex was wild with them.

Another time, my pastor's friend had me bring a woman to the convention for a pastor friend. So I brought a friend of mine who was a teacher. They took all sorts of nude pictures. He promised to send her money every month. When he failed to keep his promise, she mailed the photos to him at his home. He and his wife divorced as a result of the incident.

I pray each day for pastors' wives, for many of them are badly abused. They have become accustomed to a certain material lifestyle; they are insecure and because of their love for God, they silently cry inside and just hang in there. Their husbands are emotionally detached from them. These good and godly women waste their whole lives with 'low down' and 'down low' men who hide behind the cloth.

During my fourth marriage, I joined a small church in Los Angeles. My husband encouraged me to join the church. He would meet me there. We always drove separate cars. The pastor tried to hit on me on many occasions.

Regarding my five husbands, Dr. Juanita Bynum, I do understand "No More Sheets." When the temple leaders brought the woman to Jesus who had committed adultery, what did He say? *"He who has not sinned, let him cast the first stone."* We all live in a glass house. None of us can afford to throw a stone. It takes two to fornicate or commit adultery.

You may ask the question, "How can she share such personal information, especially being a pastor?" Well, I am telling you who I **used** to be; I am **not** that woman anymore. In the Woman, Thou Art Loosed movement, women have come out of many bondages, but never have any admitted to affairs with pastors. As the old folks used to say, "I have moved off of Broadway, and I am living on Straight Street now!" Like the Apostle Paul in the Bible, my strength and encouragement is found in Philippians, 3:13–14, which reads:

"Brethren, I count not myself to have apprehended; but this one thing I do, forgetting those things which are behind and reaching forth unto those things which are before. I press towards the mark for the prize of the high calling of God in Christ Jesus."

The hard question for you and for me is, how did I get here? By this, I mean, how did I manage to get myself in such bad situations with my husbands? I grew up in the church, but I had no understanding about my body being a temple of God. I never considered the fact that my body was not my own, and that I was bought with a price. Our bodies are temples of the Holy Ghost. Also in the Bible, II

Corinthians 6:19-20 states, *"What? Know ye not that your body is the temple of the Holy Ghost which is in you, which ye have of God, and ye are not your own? For ye are bought with a price; therefore, glorify God in your body, and in your spirit, which are God's."*

Being young, ignorant, and naïve can cause much pain and suffering in life and can also weigh a person down with much excess baggage. Our baggage can blind us from who we really are and our divine purpose for being born.

Sin adds so much to our baggage. From sin comes guilt, shame, bitterness, unworthiness, insecurities, lack of trust for others, etc. People seek many ways to deal with the effects caused by their baggage. Some use drugs, alcohol, etc. Others try to find refuge in the arms of men, only to discover that they have added more weight to their already heavy baggage.

Sometimes, others impose their baggage upon us. An example of such is being abandoned by your parents, being molested or raped, witnessing the abuse of your mother, etc. In addition, we pack our own baggage by being disobedient to our parents and to the Word of God.

Why is it that our parents do not just tell us about the ditches that we can fall into? Why do they just beat around the bush and talk in 'riddles.' I'm sure you've heard your parents say to you, 'Keep your dress down,' 'Don't be fast,' 'Why buy the cow when you can get the milk for free?' or 'Men don't want no ready-made family.'

Our parents and elders should just tell us the truth. They warn us about boys our age, our peers. But why don't they tell us to beware of the deacons and the pastors of our churches? Why? Parents tell their children things like, 'No man should touch you on the private parts of your body. He should not rub or fondle your breasts or kiss you on the lips. You should not sit on his lap.' Today, in our sick society, why aren't we teaching our girls about inappropriate sexual behavior and conduct?

As I look back over my life, I ponder this question: Why did I allow these preachers to violate me? Was it the mega bucks? Was it that they made me feel so special by sending limousines to pick me up and putting me up in nice hotels and flying me across the country? Was it my fault or theirs? Did they take advantage of my innocence and naivety?

Whatever the answers are, I was left with much baggage. This baggage could have had a lot to do with my choices of husbands. I do not have the answers for the past. What I can tell you is this—only God can rid you of your baggage, create a new you, and put the right spirit back into you.

The following passage of Scripture comes from St. Luke 13:10–13. I often asked the question, Lord, if You did it for her, why can't You do it for me? *"And He was teaching in one of the synagogues on the Sabbath. And, behold, there was a woman, which had a spirit of infirmity eighteen years, and was bowed together, and could not in no wise lift up herself. And when Jesus saw her, he called her to him, and said unto her, 'Woman, thou art loosed from thine infirmity.' And he laid his hand on her, and immediately she was made straight, and glorified God."*

Now sit back as I take you on the journey of my life and witness how I, through Christ Jesus, transformed my life with the help of God Almighty—**To God Be The Glory!**

Introduction

I WAS A YOUNG COUNTRY girl with a lot of personality, a girl who had lived a somewhat sheltered life in Opelousas, Baton Rouge, and Washington, Louisiana. I was born in New Orleans, Louisiana, but all that I know about New Orleans is what I learned from the stories told to me. I can remember growing up as the only little girl in the house with my two adult aunts who were in college, studying to be teachers, and my mother, who was also in college, studying to be a teacher. My life seemed normal (whatever that may be). I went to school, church, and played. When you are innocent and just don't know about 'stuff,' sometimes it's good. Knowing too much, seeing too much can be painful. However, pain is also a part of growing.

Moving to California in May 1968 was one hell of an experience. I thought I was learning too much when I was in Louisiana growing up around adults, but man, I have been on a roller coaster ride since my stay in California for the last 34 years. I have been falsely accused, lived the wild life, been married five times, including being in an abusive (both physical and mental) marital relationship, been swindled out of my real estate, as well as real estate and personal property willed to me, been lied to, worked hard, been competitive, learned more about Jesus, had good jobs, was a single parent, been without, got put out, realized that I really didn't know who I was, almost lost my job due to envy and strife, lost my grandmother, lost my brother, suffered through a terrible accident involving one of my daughters, lost my stepfather, was preyed upon by gigolo men, then experienced the worst thing possible—the murder of my firstborn son. I also lost a good friend (Pa) who was a soldier for the Lord. Like the biblical patriarch Job, I have often wondered how he (or I) could stand all the suffering.

As you read, you will see that in all my bad experiences, there was some good in them. Learning about Jesus has been the most refreshing thing that has ever happened to me. That's the reason I have healed the way that I did. It's all about 'The Almighty One, Jesus.' As you read this story, don't criticize, don't point the finger, and please don't judge me. **All** of us have a story. We all live in a glass house, so none of us can throw any stones. Healing is a process.

Different names are used to protect the privacy of individuals in this story. You will read where I've experienced a lot of struggles, much sin, and quite a bit of stress.

I did not plan leaving California, but I was obedient to God. To God be the glory. I experienced difficult times when I first reached my new destination, Georgia. I was there approximately one year before I found a job. It was not because I was lacking education or experience. However, I kept praising Him, regardless of my situation, because I remembered that it was He who had given me my assignment to leave California. As the songwriter says, "We fall down, but we get up." So true.

Chapter 1

My Sad, Fast Exit from Louisiana

WHEN I WAS IN ELEVENTH grade, I lived with my maternal grandmother in Opelousas, Louisiana, but I attended school in the town of Washington. I was a very petite 5-foot-plus girl, who weighed approximately 70–75 lbs. I was a somewhat happy country girl (or a small girl living in the country). Everyday, my homeroom teacher picked me up and brought me home to my aunt's very comfortable four-bedroom brick house. The house had two bathrooms, a living room, and a huge family room with beautiful tile on the floor and nice throw rugs on top of that.

My aunt had left and gone to California to live. My father and mother were separating, and believe it or not, I did not understand what was going on. I knew momma was leaving. She left on the Greyhound bus and went to California in hopes of making our lives better.

My life changed. I would not be going to our home in Baton Rouge anymore on the weekends and going to Opelousas during the week. I would have to stay with my maternal grandmother. Why? I didn't know and didn't care. I never asked any questions about what was going on. All I knew was momma was leaving, and soon, I would join her in the big, sunny state of California.

During this time, I had a boyfriend who I liked very much. We were crazy about each other. He lived in a really rural part of Washington. I was so happy when my home room teacher said I could ride with him to school. My grandmother paid him biweekly for my rides. Because of my home room teacher, I got to see my boyfriend every day. On weekends, he would go and dig worms for fishermen, who would pay him. With that money, he would catch a taxi to see me. We sat and watched the black-and-white TV. My boyfriend was 6 feet tall and good-looking. He was also the apple of my eye. In our young love, we had promised each other that we would be together the rest of our lives.

On Sundays, my grandmother and I caught a ride to the city to attend Little Zion Missionary Baptist Church (MBC), where I was baptized under the leadership of Rev. C.J. Boswell. All of my maternal family members attended this church. During the week, I attended Paul Lawrence Dunbar High School. In the evenings, I did my homework, ate, maybe washed dishes, watched TV, talked on the telephone, then went to bed. On Saturdays, I sold pecan candy that my grandmother made, fed the chickens, talked on the telephone when I could get the line (we had an eight-party telephone line), and then went to bed. There were no secrets in the community. Everybody knew everyone's business, because someone would manage to eavesdrop on the phone conversations all the time. In the late 1960s in the rural part of Opelousas, there was no such thing as a private, one-party phone line.

I was a junior in high school and was very happy. I made very good grades, I was on the honor roll, and I took college preparatory classes. My homeroom teacher, Dr. Charles Bryant, was also my speech and drama coach. He made sure that his class did very well. And I will never forget Mr. Nuhum Aldridge, our principal. I thought he was the meanest man I had ever known. My classes were Algebra, Chemistry, English, P.E., band, speech, and drama. My junior year was the bomb. I was involved in preparing for the Junior-Senior Prom. I had a leading role in the play *A Raisin in the Sun*, where I played Beneatha. We won first place locally, and then went to the state finalist competition at Grambling State University. This was really exciting. I got a chance to leave home and go to another town in northern Louisiana. We took 1st place in the contest. Grandmother had given me **that long talk** and the **Don't Do List** before I left. I also played the B flat clarinet, the alto clarinet, and the xylophone in the band. That meant for all the football games, I had to be there. Grandmother was not too thrilled about what she called my 'tramping down the street' for these school functions.

I think my grandmother had gotten enough of me 'lollygagging' down the road, because after the Junior-Senior Prom, she said she was tired of me 'ripping and running,' and informed me that I needed to be with my mother.

Every month I had to prove to my grandmother that I was having my menstrual cycle. She would actually have me pull my panties down to see evidence that it was happening. (Grandmother was not one for any foolishness.) She was responsible for me, and she tried to make sure that everything was all right, as best she knew.

Oddly, I never heard from my daddy or my paternal grandmother. They were right in Baton Rouge, about an hour away from where I stayed. I did not call them, either. It's sad that children feel the pain of parents separating and really not know what's going on. My parents owned a very large club/restaurant called the Bamboo Seafood Inn. It was probably the largest club in the city at that time. The club had Blues singer Ko-Ko Taylor and other singing artists who performed. I was a very young waitress there, only 14-years-old. One night I decided to take a drink with a 21-year-old man. I believe he put some drug in my drink that night, because even though I had drunk alcohol before, I had never felt like that. Anyway, I remember the security guard came to the car with a flashlight and took me back into the club. We had living quarters in the rear of the building. Nothing bad happened that night. My mother and aunt used to make me wear panties and a girdle, they said it was lady-like. I think that man had intentions of molesting or raping me. When the guard brought me in, instead of talking to me to find out what I could tell them about the incident, my mother's sister started beating me with a broom. I could not even feel the licks, I was so out of it. I recall my daddy telling my aunt that if she hit me one more time, he was going to take the broom and strike her. That's when she stopped.

My mother was a teacher, and my father was a contractor/construction worker. Momma taught elementary school in a small city called Plaisance, in the outskirts of Opelousas. At that time, some schools were from the first to the eighth grade, and others were from the first to the twelfth grade. Momma taught at one with all the grades. She was a very good teacher, both for her class children and for her own children. I really hated to see momma leave, but she did what she had to do to make things right for herself and her three children.

I remember momma taking my brothers and me with her to the after-school activities, like football and basketball games, dances, track meets, and so forth. I enjoyed the big popcorn balls made with delicious maple syrup, tasty potato pies that were called 'niggers in a blanket,' fried chicken sandwiches, hot chili, chili cheese dogs, and oh man, those delicious, juicy hamburgers made with lettuce and tomatoes. The food was good with hot chocolate and strawberry sodas.

Before I left Louisiana, my boyfriend asked me to marry him. I agreed. He gave me an engagement ring and promised that after graduation from school the following year, he would come meet me, and we would be together the rest of our lives. That sounded so good. Then the weekend came, and my maternal uncle, who was a very prominent pastor in Baton

Rouge, came and got me in Opelousas. I left with my uncle. My boyfriend and I both cried. We hated to leave each other. Daddy lived in Baton Rouge, not too far from my uncle. I never even had a chance to say good-bye to him. I flew from New Orleans to Los Angeles, May 28, 1968. Momma picked me up from LAX airport, and my life began anew in California.

Chapter 2

Life in Southern California

IT WAS A BEAUTIFUL DAY when the airplane landed in Los Angeles, California. The flight was smooth. It was my first time ever flying. I was scared. I prayed. I wanted to see and be with my momma, but I passionately hated being separated from my one and only love back in Louisiana. Momma and my aunt met me at the airport. We hugged and kissed. She was happy to see me, and I was happy to be with her. She took me on a little tour from the airport on our way home to Normandie Ave. I had butterflies in my stomach. Coming from rural Louisiana, I was really afraid of the bright lights in the big city.

When we got to the house, momma showed me my room. She also showed me her room, which was in the rear of the house. Then she told me that I had a room-mate. I did not like the idea of having a roommate, but what could I say. My roommate was a girl about my age. She had a brother, who also lived with my mother. I could not understand why. I told momma that I would be spending a lot of time in the room with her because I did not like the idea of a roommate, especially one I did not know. I really did not like the idea of sharing a room with anyone, because I was use to the privacy of my own room. My aunt in whose beautiful home I lived in Opelousas was also living with us.

Mamma showed me around the huge house, which had four big bedrooms, a large living room, dining room, kitchen, and a breakfast room off the kitchen, a service porch, and two bathrooms. It was different from the type of homes I had lived in. Mamma called my younger auntie that had been living in California, and who was somewhat established. Her place was right around the corner. Momma instructed me on how to get there, so I walked over to see her. I was afraid, but I went. I spoke to people whom I passed and said, "How you doing Ma'am?" or "Sir?" The people looked at me like I was an alien. I felt really strange. *Had I done something wrong? No, this place*, which I thought was paradise on earth, *had strange people, people that were different from me*. People living here did not speak to strangers. I had been taught to speak to people; in fact, I was taught to speak to everyone. *Oh, well*, I thought, *what's next?* When I got to my auntie's, I was very happy. We used to talk on the telephone all the time when I was down South. She was real upbeat. I liked her very much. We talked and talked and laughed and had a good day. Momma came and met me at her house, then we walked home.

School was still in session when I arrived in California. Momma was teaching in Compton during the day, and she taught at Washington Adult School, in Los Angeles, two nights a week. On the weekends, she also worked at White Front Store. Momma was a workaholic. She wanted the best for my brothers and me. I went with her a few days on her day job. I was very inquisitive and wanted to know where I would attend school, if I would be graduating, and if the school would accept my classes. Would I be able to get a job? Would my boyfriend still come to this place? I was overflowing with questions.

I finally met the brother of my roommate. He was attending school and held an evening job. Mamma introduced me to him. Soon he asked me to go on a date to the drive-in movies. I remember talking to my boyfriend, who I left back home. I really don't recall how it happened, but I either took the iniative and sent his ring back to him, or he asked me for it. But, in August, I sent him the ring. Soon after that, I heard that he was getting married. My feelings were hurt a little, but I got over it. Of course, I had also gone on a date with my roommate's brother.

In June 1968, I wanted a job so badly. Everyone in the house was motivated and had jobs. My oldest brother was in the USMC, playing in the band in El Toro, California. I applied for a summer youth program; at that time, it was called the NYC (National Youth Corp). I had to take a test and—thank God—I passed it. I worked for the IRS downtown Los Angeles. My mother would drop me off and pick me up. I wanted to experience riding the bus, but soon, that was too slow for me. I asked momma to take me to get my driver's license. Driver's Education was a requirement in the schools in Opelousas, Louisiana, so therefore, I already knew how to drive. I had learned to drive on a four-speed car. My only problem and fear was driving in Southern California. Well, I got my license and momma let me drive her Lemas Pontiac. While she was working one day, her car was stolen. I wondered who could be so evil to take her car. Well, she got a rental car, but I could not drive it. I went to work everyday and was very happy. Our youth supervisor was Mr. Tommy Hawkins. Every Friday, we did something fun away from the job. It seemed like I might kind of like this place after all.

My momma was very proud of me. I earned my own money and was looking forward to my senior year here in this big city. I was indeed intimidated by my surroundings, but I was ready to take on this new challenge. I ask momma to send for the senior class ring I had ordered with my class in Washington, Louisiana. Unfortunately, my principal there stated that they were going to refund my deposit, because they did not think I wanted that ring after I left. I was disappointed, but got over it.

I told momma I wanted to be an actress. This place was so big, I didn't know where to get started. Momma took me around a few places; she then enrolled me in modeling classes. The school tried to make me feel inferior. As they were showing me how to put on makeup (which I had never worn), they informed me that black people had big lips, and that I should put lip liner on to make my lips smaller. (Now people are getting their lips sized larger; big lips are gorgeous.) They also taught posture techniques and instructed on how to be a lady.

Soon I was sent to another agency. Believe me, I was scared. I was running in the fast lane. I took a series of pictures for a profile. An agency called for an interview. Momma took me there. After arriving, a man told me to take off all of my clothes and come out for photo shoot. I pretended to go to the dressing room, but instead, ran straight out of the building. That ended my modeling career. I did not return to the modeling classes. *Didn't they know that I was a very shy girl and was not about to reveal my body that way?* Momma had signed a contract at the modeling school, so she had to pay off the balance. I called a few actors and actresses to make job inquiries, but they let me know calling them was not the way into Hollywood. I had it all wrong, thinking that by just being in California would make it easy to get into the acting business.

Momma enrolled me in the nearby high school, which was Manual Arts High School. They checked my records from Louisiana and found I had enough credits to graduate in one semester. I had to take only three required classes—CAP & G, U.S. History, and Senior Composition. The principal was concerned with me graduating at sixteen because of 'immaturity on my part,' so he said. I'm so glad that my momma did not go for that crap. She told him she felt I could handle it.

I had a very nice counselor, Ms. Patricia Wainwright, who helped me. I did have a problem getting a required class. The history classes were filled, so I enrolled in a night school class. The late Ms. Georgia Maryland was my teacher. She had me scared that I was not going to pass her class. I studied very hard and did extra work so I could graduate. I also took Senior Composition, CAP & G, Physical Education, and Home Economics. My home economics teacher was very nice and patient with me. I was a country girl, afraid to sew. My grandmother had done all the sewing, washing, ironing, and cooking for me. Mrs. Eula Ingram was my teacher, and in later years, she became my co-worker at Manual Arts H.S. My counselor had once asked me what my goals were. I responded that I wanted to come back to Manual Arts to teach.

Momma got me situated in school, after I had finished work that summer. Recall that I had a roommate, who had a brother sharing our home. We all were attending the same school, and we all got closer. My roommate had a boyfriend, and I started dating her brother, James. He had four classes, then in the afternoon, he went to work. That work experience counted as a class. We went on a few dates. He had a car, so occasionally, I rode with him to school. Other days I walked. He was a senior. Graduation came around and both of us graduated. He had print shop classes, so he made our class graduation announcements. I graduated with a 3.9, in the top 10 percent of the last winter class at Manual Arts H. S. I received a silver-seal metal for my accomplishments at sixteen years old.

I was granted a full four-year scholarship to the University in Evanston, Illinois, but I did not want to go. I cried and cried. I told momma she was just trying to get rid of me. I was afraid to leave. Also, I had lost my first boyfriend back home by moving to California. I did not want to lose my new friend by relocating out of state. I had just started dating this young man. Momma gave in and told me I did not have to leave.

A new semester had begun. I had no intentions on going anywhere. Momma woke me up and yelled at me a few times. She told me there was a college in the city of Compton where she worked, and that I was going to go to a school somewhere. I got up, went to, and enrolled in Compton Junior College, along with my boyfriend, James. I was told college was a little more difficult than high school. I spoke to a counselor, got my schedule of classes, and started school.

During the time between high school graduation and starting college, my momma married the late Isaac Nelson. He was a wonderful man. He bought me my first car. By now, my younger brother was attending Normandie Elementary School, and my older brother was in the Marines. Momma and my stepfather bought a three-bedroom home in Compton, and we all moved. I loved our new home. I had my own bedroom, while my brothers shared. The bedrooms had intercoms. I remember my brothers would wake up very early, then wake me by calling me out of my name over the intercom.

I went to school and worked at Sears, on Vermont and Slauson, in Los Angeles. James and I continued to date. I attended Compton Junior College one semester, then enrolled in Pepperdine College in August of that same year. I planned to get out of school quickly by attending both colleges. I was now seventeen-years-old. I took 30–36 units a trimester/semester. At the age of twenty, I had graduated, married, and was teaching at Bethune Junior High School.

Chapter 3

Seduction

WHEN I ARRIVED IN SOUTHERN California, the members of my family had joined a large MBC church. I started attending faithfully and later joined it, too. The minister took a special interest in me. *Why?* I wondered. My experiences that resulted from the interaction with this pastor have been very difficult for me to write about because of a great deal of guilt and shame. With much grief, I confess that ***I was my pastor's mistress and that I was a madam for other pastors***.

After joining the church, the pastor had an associate minister call me and ask me to come see him. I told him I was new in town and did not know my way around. *What on God's earth could this man want with me?* I thought. I had learned to trust ministers and pastors. My uncle and grandfather were ministers. We use to have the ministers over to our house on Sundays for a meal.

One night, the pastor called and sent a limo to pick me up from my parents' house in Compton. I was nervous, but went. When I reached my destination, then I *really* wondered why he wanted to see me at the LAX Hilton Hotel.

Not only was my pastor sitting in the plush suite with half a gallon of liquor on the table, drinking while listening to the blues, but also several other well-known pastors in the city were doing likewise. I really felt out of place and misled. It was awkward, but I stayed to find out what was going on. This was a man I respected and looked up to regarding my religious beliefs. He had been teaching me the Scriptures. I had put him on a pedestal. Oh, how I enjoyed him preaching and singing. Now I felt crestfallen. I asked why I was there. He replied, "Well, daughter, you are a chosen one. Consider yourself as cream of the crop." Then he asked me what I wanted to eat and drink, that I could order anything I wanted on the menu. So I did. Man, that was nice and fancy. He gave me a $100 bill and told me he'll see me another time. I left and was taken home by the associate minister. Neither of us spoke in the car.

Starting at the age of 17, I served as his mistress. The next time I was summoned was on a Saturday night. (You know, the night before Sunday's church service.) The party was on and jumping by the time I got there. It was a different hotel located on Century Blvd., this time. Again, there was plenty of liquor, snacks, music, other ministers, and women. We all partied, and I had a buzz. We used to dance to BB King, Bobby Bland, Aretha Franklin, Luther Vandross, The Chilites, James Brown, and many others. There was Hennessy, gin & juice, wine, and also marijuana available. The pastor and I gracefully left and went to another room which was private. We got our freak on and got intimate. I could not believe it. I was in total shock. I told him that I did not believe this was happening. He responded by saying that he was a man before being a pastor, and his penis gets hard just like any other man's. When I left, he gave me two $100 bills and told me to buy myself something nice.

When he summoned and I did not show up, he told me he was disappointed, and that I must have been with someone else. He said, "Don't play with me that way." He gave me the name 'Runaway.' I told him that he was wrong, and that I did not have a male in my life at that time.

Later, all this became commonplace and good. The reverend would go out-of-town for revivals and fly me over to meet him. We would have lunch and/or dinner, ..., then I would get dressed and be in church for the service. We never flew on the same flight coming or going on our clandestine encounters.

Soon his pastoral friends that he partied with asked me to invite some of my female friends, which I did. They gave me money for doing so. When out-of-town ministers visited, he paid me to get clients for them also. They came from Texas, Louisiana, Illinois, as well as California. We all played cards, dominoes, drank, smoked, danced, and had wild, freaky sex.

Once I brought one of my relatives. She had a nice figure. As soon as we entered the room, those men acted like hungry dogs. They started grabbing on her, feeling her breasts, and acted like dogs in heat. She looked at me in amazement; I looked back at her and shrugged my shoulders. She soon got in the grove with everybody else. The ministers were so happy that night, they all gave me a nice piece of change (large bills). When I found out that she only received $50 and I told her what I received, she was upset with me. Those men partied harder than a person in the nightclub and were wilder than people that do not attend church. If a girl were on her monthly cycle and tried to beg off from sex, they simply said, "What kind of blood don't wash off?"

The penthouse was not uncommon for them to rent. We shared the jacuzzi and the rooms. On a few occasions, I ran into other female members from the church. They would either be leaving when I was entering or entering when I was leaving. If I chose to stay the night, he gave me my own room.

On one occasion, I took a female to meet an out-of-town minister. She took all kinds of photos with him and kept them. He promised to send her money and send for her to come to his hometown. He was stupid. He gave her his correct address and telephone number at church and at home. He did not live up to his promises, so she blackmailed him and sent the pictures to his home. She was single and had nothing to loose. I do believe he must have gone through a very bad time with his wife.

My pastor told me that he carried a gun and would use it, if he had to. I know that he was not lying, because I ask him to see it and he showed it to me.

Once he was not present at a hotel when one of his friends called and told me to come over. I did. When I arrived, this friend tried to proposition me with kibbles and bits and wanted me to promise never to tell the pastor. He was scared for his life, afraid that I would tell the pastor, especially when I would not go along with his game.

After James and I separated, I knew where I could go. I knew who I could call. The hotel doors were still open.

I finally woke up one day and said this was wrong. I'm glad that chapter of my life is over. Years later, after my life had changed, I recall speaking to one of these pastors with whom I had been involved and told him that I was pastoring my own church. He cursed me and said, "Ain't no damn woman got no business pastoring. She cannot baptize members when she is on her period." Then he remarked, "The door is still open for you with me." I did not respond to him, because I also know that the door to hell is still open, too.

Chapter 4

My School Life

My senior year at Manual Arts High School was as much fun as it could be. I was quiet. I was alone. I missed being at home back in Louisiana with the people I knew. It was not the same. My high school there was big; but Manual Arts was too big. The students were much different in California than those in Louisiana. Where I grew up, everybody knew everybody—but not here. I didn't mix with my peers. I stayed around my teachers and studied. James and I used to eat lunch together. Some days, I would go to his classroom to watch him on the printing machine, which I found fascinating. I had never seen anything like it before. James liked me, and I liked him a lot. He didn't talk much, but around him, I talked too much.

At that time, all I did was go to school and work. My goal was to get out of school quickly. My classes were so easy for me. I passed all of them with As, Bs, and one C. We had a prom, but I decided not to go. James had to work that night, and since I did not know anyone, I chose not to go. My biggest adventure was looking forward to graduating from high school.

On graduating night, January 30, 1969, I was soooo happy.

My mother's expectations were high, so I had to go to college and get a degree. She and both of her sisters were teachers. My biological father's sister (Aunt Sweetie) was a teacher/librarian, also. You may have surmised by now that going to college was not an option for me. I received a four-year, fully paid scholarship at the University in Evanston, Illinois, in Speech and Drama. I did not want to go there. That meant leaving my momma and my new boyfriend. When I finished crying and carrying on, telling momma that she was trying to get rid of me, and that I didn't know anyone there, she decided to let me stay home. But she told me I was going to college. She was not kidding, and I knew it. She was very serious. Monday morning arrived, and she woke me up early to enroll at Compton Junior College.

I had really good teachers my first semester. I took Psychology, English Grammar & Composition, P.E., Biology, Introduction to Sociology, and Introduction to Music. Many people told me to stay away from the students' lounge, because if you hang out there, it could become 'contagious.' I went by a couple of times. People were playing card games, dominos, talking on the pay telephones, with plenty of socializing taking place. A lightbulb flashed in my head that warned, "Oh no, stay out of there. Stay focused. You have a goal to achieve. You can not do it by being in the lounge." I heeded the warning and stayed away. I applied for and got a teacher's aide job with Los Angeles Unified School District. I worked at Markham

Junior High several days a week after I left the junior college, and I also worked at Sears (at Vermont & Slauson) part-time. After one semester at Compton J.C., I enrolled in Pepperdine College in Los Angeles, August 1970. At that time I was steadily dating my boyfriend, James, who attended Compton J.C., and who also worked in Burbank in the evening. When I enrolled in Pepperdine, the college situation was different from what I was used to. This school was a private, expensive, predominately Caucasian one. Momma signed for me to get a student loan.

My classes were geared towards speech and drama because I was still set on a major in acting. I attended the first trimester, which was a truly rude awakening in so many ways. The instructors were very different, although I had some very good ones. Chapel attendance several days a week was mandatory, as were religion classes.

Even though I did well at Compton Junior College, I received one fail, two Ds, and one C my first trimester at Pepperdine. I was embarrassed and humiliated. I knew my momma was going to lay hands on me for sure when she found out about my grades, so I did not tell her. Instead, I eloped and left home. Yes, I did. I married James. My older brother, Jr., helped me do all of the dirty work. We got married at a wedding chapel on Vermont Ave., called Bride's Choice Wedding Chapel.

Momma was so hurt, she did not know what to do. I pretended that I did not care, but I was so scared. She did not yet have my grades. The worst was yet to come.

For our honeymoon, James took a vacation, and we went to Louisiana to meet his mother for Christmas. By the time we returned from Louisiana, my grades had arrived. I was forced to listen to momma's sermon about me going to school. She did not care if I was married or not, **I was going to get an education**. James also informed me he was not planning on having a dumb wife. *Okay*, I thought, *that was it. I did not die.* I was yelled at, but I survived it. Now it was time for me to buckle down. When I signed up for my classes at Pepperdine, I also received a letter that I was on academic probation. I continued to take classes at both schools and work. That next trimester, I earned four As and one B. My grade point average was not strong enough to take me off probation. I stayed on it for three trimesters, which was equivalent to one year. That motivated me to study, study, and study some more.

I pledged in a sorority at Pepperdine called the KKK (Kappa Kappa Kappa). It was fun. I had to do all my initiation on campus. I stayed away from home on campus a few days. I was so glad I did not have to live on campus. That experience was really not for me.

I kept in touch with my counselors at both schools in order to see what courses I needed for graduation from each school. I was so happy in February 1972, when I earned an A.A. degree from Compton Junior College, and August 1972, when I earned a Bachelor's Degree from Pepperdine College.

Chapter 5

My First Marriage

ON DECEMBER 14, 1970, I ELOPED with my first love here in Los Angeles, California. I was 18 years old and James was 21. He was a handsome, six-foot, brown-skinned, strong black man. We were married for twelve years. He was my high school sweetheart and a neat freak; everything had to be in order. He kept the lawn beautiful. He maintained the cars. He used to drink and tell me that nice ladies stay at home while men go out on the town. Yes, we were married for 12 years; however, longevity in a marriage is no signal for a happy marriage. I had 12 years of being mentally and physically abused. He pulled a gun on me three separate occasions, and thank God, I am still alive to tell about it.

During our twelve years of marriage, we were separated three times. After the birth of our third child, I told God, if He let me get away this time, I would not look back. My baby, Michael, was only two-weeks-old when I left him for the last time.

We got a one-bedroom apartment in Compton. James had his car, and I had mine. We were both working, and I was going to school. My aspirations were to finish school and become an actress. My older brother liked James; they became friends. My now deceased brother, Sululah Jr., had a celebration for us. He bought food and liquor for the celebration. He knew a gentleman who lived near Pepperdine, and this man allowed us to have a small celebration at his house. Sululah had a very sweet personality; to know him was to love him. He was mischievous, but at the same time, he had a heart of gold. I loved my brother. After I got married, I still did not know how to cook, wash, iron, or sew. When I cooked breakfast the day after our marriage, I burned both the bacon and eggs. James sweetly said that it was very good. Everything I cooked was either undercooked or overcooked. One day he decided to teach me the basics of cooking.

When James got his vacation during the month of December, we drove to Baton Rouge, Louisiana. My biological father lived only two blocks from James' mother. When we arrived, my husband got a very warm reception from his family. I got a breath of coldness that I was not anticipating from his mother, sisters, and brothers. I was disappointed. I went to see my daddy (Sululah Milow Sr.), the peanut man, who lived three streets away. He has been selling peanuts since the age of 12 or 13; he now is 82-years-old. He always had a very loud voice. I was very fearful of the tone of his voice. He told me I should not have gotten married so soon, then he asked why I rushed to do so. He stated, "You don't know anything about the family you've married off into, but since you have gotten married, try to make the best of it."

I also went to see my paternal grandmother, the late Bessie Milo (Ma Bessie). She did not talk much. She was a very neat lady, who kept her kitchen spotless. I enjoyed watching her. She took so much pride in all that she did. She even ironed her sheets and tablecloths. While I was there, she washed my clothes and cooked for me.

I traveled to visit my maternal great-great-aunt in Opelousas named Ella Fisher. She loved me so much; she always thought I was an angel. She bought my first piano and taught me how to pray on my knees. When I was living in Louisiana, I would go to New Orleans every year and stay with her. She was a good, old, Southern Christian. She had an old-fashion record player and used to play Mahalia Jackson songs. Every Wednesday night, the two of us would have our prayer meeting, where we would sing songs, read the Bible, and pray. She wished James and I well in our marriage and told us that if we did not have a disagreement, we would be living a lie. She explained, "No two people can live under the same roof all the time and agree to everything all the time." Aunt Ella and her husband Uncle Fisher were married for fifty-one years, then he passed away. After that, she moved to Opelousas, where she had been born and still owned property.

Aunt Ella told us we needed to pray, and pray without ceasing. She also informed me that she was going to give me a down payment on a home. She believed that since we were married, James and I should have a home. "If you have children, they should be brought up in a home, with a yard and plenty of space," was her philosophy.

James stayed with his relatives during that time, and I stayed with mine. That was **not** a very good start for our marriage. When it was time for us to leave, we said our good-byes and left. On the way home, he remained silent. When we arrived, my goal was to locate the right home for us to purchase. Mr. Bill Bagby, a very nice man who had no hands, helped us find a lovely, three-bedroom home with a fireplace in Compton. Aunt Ella sent me the money, as she promised, then we moved.

Mother gave us furniture to help us get started, and I continued my schooling and working.

Then my mother-in-law started calling collect, asking my husband for money to help with her bills. It would have been okay with me, but I minded the person-to-person collect calls to him. Previously, he had admonished me that his money was **his**, and my money was **ours**. Whenever his mother or any of his family members called collect, James ordered me to accept the calls. That was not a very good feeling. I ended up working for us, and he was working for his family and himself. This went on almost every month. He took my checks and gave me an allowance.

James had a younger brother that got into mischief quite a bit. When his mother called, wanting this brother to come live with us, I refused. This is when James began abusing me. He screamed at me, and I screamed at him. My aunt had not helped us buy a house in order to fill it with his siblings or my in-laws. He slapped me so hard that I saw stars and stripes. He was six feet and weighed 180 lbs; I was 5 feet 2 and weighed 90–95 lbs. There was no need to try to fight him—I would have been fighting a losing battle. Problems had begun. I was told once your spouse hits you, it becomes easier and easier the next time. James told me he would never strike me again. I continued with school. When the telephone bill arrived every month, the weekly—now secret—collect phone calls appeared.

Summer came along with two of James' siblings. One stayed with us, sporting an attitude. The other one stayed with her in-laws. I tried to do everything possible to make my sister-in-law happy, but she had been programmed too well to change her behavior. For seven days, our home was filled with tension. But I got over that. My husband and I did not speak for three or four weeks. Whenever I would attempt to talk with him, he would get up and walk past me, as if I did not exist.

One day during my last trimester in school, his family called. His brother had shot his little sister in the head. I told him to take our credit card and purchase a ticket to fly home. The family called collect almost every hour. The boy took the three-year-old sister to the hospital on a bicycle in a basket. No one knew where their mother was at the time of the accident. The three-year-old child died. I told him as soon as I completed my exams, I would meet him there, even though my in-laws did not want me around. I went to support my husband. When I arrived, I was treated as if I had done something wrong. James would leave me at the house while he and his mother did errands. His siblings had all planned to dress alike at the funeral, and they did. I was left completely out of the picture. The day of the funeral, I was not allowed to sit with my husband. Instead, I was relegated to sitting all the way in the back of the church.

When I returned home, I continued with my goal to finish school. During this time, we had tried to conceive, but were unsuccessful. I spoke to James about adopting a baby, but he adamantly refused because I would not let siblings come live in our house, so he was not about to adopt someone else's child to bring into the house.

I thank Jesus, because finally in August 1972, I graduated from Pepperdine. I was overjoyed. Immediately I began searching for a better job. I took the probation officers' written test, where I scored 95/100. Unfortunately, I did not get that job. I did the required student teaching, one semester at Bret Harte Junior High and a semester at Gardena High School. Then I had a job interview at Jordan High School. The interview went fine, but as I left the school, a male student approached me, thinking I was a student also. He asked, "What's up, baby?" I was twenty-years-old, and these kids were 15 years to 18 years old. Teaching high school was not on my agenda at that time. I drove around the city, spotted a really nice-looking school on 69th and Broadway. I stopped, and inquired if I could speak with the principal. Even though I had no appointment scheduled with her, she agreed to see me. Guess what? She hired me. I was twenty, excited, and I thanked Jesus for leading me to this opportunity.

Chapter 6

My First Teaching Assignment

THE DAY WAS JANUARY 29, 1973; MRS. Dora Ballard had hired me to teach Special Ed transitional students at Mary McCloud Bethune Junior High School. I was so happy and excited. My beginning salary was a whopping $800 a month. This was so nice. I had a real job, working with children. Mrs. Ballard was a very smart and very strict lady. I was hired as a long-term substitute. In order to become a probationary teacher, I had to take the required test. During the course of that first semester, I took and passed the test.

Mrs. Ballard would often come to my classroom unannounced to observe me. She carried her notebook and pen. She would nod her head as if to say 'continue' while I taught. At the end of the workday, I went to her office for the evaluation. I was so scared when I went there, that I was shaking in my shoes and sweating in my palms. She always told me that I was doing a fine job. Mrs. Ballard was always so quiet and professional. She reminded me of momma.

I left home at 6 A.M. to get to work early, but I always stopped at my momma's house first. We would have coffee or hot chocolate together every morning. Then I arrived at school between 7:00–7:15, read my Bible, eat breakfast, and prepare for my students. On Saturdays, I shopped and cleaned my house. My husband went out on Friday nights, but refused to take me with him because 'nice ladies stay home.' Only men hang out. He had double standards. He would not even take me out to dinner unless it was an anniversary or birthday. He said it was better to eat at home. On Sundays, I would attend church alone. Soon I found a lady minister who pastored a small church and began attending there. I started going to the Friday night services, which lasted 4–5 hours. James did not believe I was attending church. He followed me a few times, although I was not aware of it. I invited him to church services; one night, out of curiosity, he came. The evangelist was also a prophet. She had James stand and told him he had plans to leave his wife. She proceeded to tell him that he would be like a fish on dry land, struggling to get to water. Afterwards, he sat down. This evangelist spoke to people in a manner that only that person understood what she was talking about. That particular night, she told me she saw me rocking my own little baby. I laughed because the doctors had told me I was not going to have any children.

I was so in love with children that I would occasionally bring them home with me from school. I had one little girl, Yvonne, who thought I was her momma. She even called me momma. Yvonne would come to my house at least three times a week and every weekend. She was at my house when a long distant collect call came from one of James' sisters. James was on the telephone, unaware that Yvonne was also. She eavesdropped on the conversation. James' sister told him he could not tell anyone what she was about to say, and that the brother who had shot their little sister had raped both of her children.

Yvonne then asked me to take her to McDonald's, so I did. She told me about the conversation, then begged me not to say anything. I did not say anything while she was there.

James had his own way of doing things. The following week, he asked if his brother could live with us. I refused and told him he did not even know his brother, because they had never really lived together. I got beat up again. James gave me a black eye. One of my friends in the teachers' lounge asked me if I ran into the doorknob. I responded that I ran into my husband's fist. Then I went to my classroom feeling depressed. After that, there was more silent treatment for a few weeks at home.

The summer came and in July, I flew to Louisiana with my now deceased stepfather. He stayed in a hotel, while I stayed with my biological father and Ma Bessie. I did not visit my in-laws at all. The two of us stayed about ten days. My uncle, who was a minister, and my stepfather were very close. My stepfather would fried fish with some of my uncle's friends, then bring the catch home, clean them, and eat fried fish at my uncle's house.

In the early 1970s, my late uncle would allow me to speak at his church, Star Hill MBC, in Baton Rouge, Louisiana. The trip and all the good food I knew I would be eating excited me. Good Gumbo, dirty rice, barbeque, boudin, pigs' feet, ham hocks, greens, chitterlings, rice, hog cracklings, hog head cheese, etc. Well, most of the time I flew, God revealed a message to me. This particular year, I was so happy thinking about all the good food waiting for me and how I was going to pig out. But, contrary to my thoughts, God directed me to be on a seven-day fast, drinking water only. *Oh, man, why?* I thought. But I obeyed. My folks could not believe I was not eating as much as I like to eat.

That Sunday when I got to church, the anointing was so heavy, people started falling out as soon as God had me open my mouth. I do not profess to be a soloist, but as the words of the song "Only Believe," came from my mouth, the presence of the Lord was there. People were being healed, saved, delivered. I praise God for my uncle, the late, great Rev. Huey P. Greene. The Lord blessed the people that day through words of inspiration. It truly was a blessing.

In 1973 when we left Louisiana and got back home, I discovered I was three months pregnant with my first child. James and I were so happy. I was going back to my teaching job, and I was expecting a baby in February. My principal assigned me to be the drama teacher/coordinator. I put together a Thanksgiving production and also a Christmas production. They were very successful. I worked until the end of that semester, but did not return after it.

Chapter 7

My First Child

ON FEBRUARY 24, 1974, I GAVE BIRTH to a beautiful, healthy, eight-pound baby girl. My mother and my husband were there with me the whole time I was in labor. She was born on a sunny Sunday morning, very early. I thought she was not ever going to get here. I stayed in labor for sixteen hours. James and I went through our little selfish disagreement. He wanted to name her after his late little sister, Charise Antonnitte, but I refused. My aunt and I had already made up some names. James and I finally came to an agreement and named her Phamesha LaSha'.

When I got home, I was so pleased that the pregnancy was over. James was such a proud and happy father. He held the baby. She was born at Kaiser Hospital. We had rooming-in service. I could pull the special drawer out and my baby girl would be in the room with me; if I pushed the drawer in, she would be in the nursery. This gave us time to learn how to feed, bathe, and spoil her. Both of my brothers came to the hospital. They were very proud uncles and both wanted to be her godparents, so I allowed it. Phamesha had three sets of godparents.

I went through some bad postpartum blues. I was so depressed and did not want to eat. I remember my mother coming over, hand-feeding me. I developed bad hemorrhoids. But I loved my brand new, live baby doll and thanked God for giving me this wonderful bundle of joy. She was given so many gifts.

My maternal grandmother, Mo-Mo, came over. She prayed for us and told me I was not to leave my house for six weeks. Then she held the baby. Mo-Mo told me that the Lord had blessed us with a healthy baby, and we needed to live and take care of her. I stayed home until the next semester began.

Mo-Mo kept my baby girl while I was at work. I would get up extra early to stop at my momma's house, take the baby to my grandmother, and then go to work. I paid $25 a week for childcare. I did not like the idea of leaving my little princess, but I had to go to work. When I started working again, I was very happy to be receiving a full check once more. At that time, I was still allowing James to take my checks. On Saturdays, I took my baby to the Cerritos Mall. On Sundays, we attended church. In fact, after my baby's first checkup, her next stop was church. Proverbs 22:6 says, *"Train up a child in the way he should go, and when he is old he will not depart from it."* My husband did not attend church with us. When we got home from church, his friends were sitting at the dining room table, playing dominos and drinking alcohol. He expected me to fix dinner and feed everyone. I did for a while, but I felt like I was being treated like a maid. He did not appreciate me, and his friends disrespected me. After they had been drinking and my husband would go to the bathroom or be somewhere else in the house, they would always say inappropriate things to me. I complained to my husband about it, but he never believed me. I would get my baby's things ready for the next week and get myself ready for work. If James drank too much, we would argue, and I occasionally got beat again. After I decided to keep my money, James became very angry. He beat me, so I ran off with my little baby girl who was 17 months old. We lived in an apartment in the country club.

Chapter 8

The Birth of James Jr.

IN 1977, MY PRETTY LITTLE princess, Mesha, told me she wanted a sister or brother. In September that year, I enrolled in Azusa Pacific College to work on my Master's Degree in Educational Psychology. Amazingly, when school began, I was expecting our second baby. I was not discouraged with returning to school. Like David who encouraged himself in the book of Samuel from the Bible, I prayed and encouraged myself, too. James was against me going back to school. I had arguments and physical fights with him. He both physically and mentally abused me—known as domestic violence today. He told me I had enough education. *Forget him*, I thought. *I am going to school to better myself. I want more than a B.A. I really want a Ph.D. God, help me take one step at a time.* Pregnancy was not about to put a halt on me.

    James would go out and come home angry, cursing me. I was feisty and did not keep my mouth closed when he said something idiotic to me. I was not an 'okay, honey' wife. I had to say what was on my mind. I knew and believed in a Man far greater that James, who we call Jesus. I felt too Blessed to be

Stressed. This motivated me to really want to do something with my life.

While I was attending Azusa Pacific, working on my degree, I was also teaching at Bethune Junior High and taking care of my daughter. We had clusters at Azusa at the time I was attending. I thought our cluster was the best. I had classmates from Compton Unified, LA Unified, Pomona Unified, and Cerritos Unified. We really bonded and got along well.

I had a goal. My baby was on the way, I read, studied, taught school, and was beaten by James. I did all my class work, took my tests, sent my daughter to preschool, attended church, and prayed that my unborn baby would be intelligent and healthy.

I took my written exam and passed it; next, I was on a team for my oral exam and passed it. The panel team informed me I had passed and did not need to answer any more questions.

My Mesha was excited about her momma giving her a little brother or sister. Although she was only four-years-old, I know she had to have heard the arguments and fights between her daddy and me. I had a very dear friend, Annette, attending Azusa with me, who I confided with. She would listen to me and try to console me on those days I attended school crying. My face was swollen and I was feeling really hurt. She was a happily married woman. I use to listen to her talk about her life, her children, and her husband.

After taking my oral exam, I was eagerly looking forward to marching with my graduating class on May 6, 1978. I stayed on the honor roll the entire time and graduated with honors, but I could not march with the class that day because God had decided to make this day a most memorable day in my life, a day that will never be forgotten. That day, my second child, a son, was born.

Earlier, I had told James I was feeling like the time was approaching for the baby to be born. His supervisor had given him two tickets to the Anaheim Angels baseball game. We both decided that he should go to the game and if it was truly the blessed moment I anticipated, I promised to call the stadium and have him paged. Well, around 8:30 P.M., one of my girlfriends came over to be with me. We went to get some seafood. It did not stay down. I started having pains. My friend called the stadium and had James paged. They wrote on the billboard, 'James Johnson, GO HOME! URGENT.' My baby was in the spotlight already. When James got home, we rushed to Kaiser Harbor City. My eight-pound, handsome, little baby boy not only made a big scene at the Angels game, but he also made his grand entrance into this world on the day I received my master's degree (and could not be at the ceremony). On May 6, 1978, God gave me a little angel, and it seems like it was only yesterday. The doctor slapped him on his butt to make him cry. He was laid back even when he came into the world. Thank you, God, for giving my James Jr. his first breath in his tiny body.

James wanted his son to bear his name. It was alright with me. Mesha nicknamed her brother June-June. She was so happy to have a little brother 'baby doll.' My hospital stay was three days. While there, Jr. slept most of the time. I nursed him, bathed him, and changed him. He was not a whiney baby. Momma came to the hospital. She told me she knew that lil ugly baby was her grandson.

When we got home from the hospital, I experienced some very bad stomach cramping. I called my mother, and she assured me that sometimes that happens after birthing. I woke my husband up, crying, and told him not only was I cramping very badly, but I also had a temperature of 101. He retorted that all I wanted was attention. The next day, I kept complaining. When I went to the bathroom, something long and ugly fell out of me. I screamed and started shaking. I called James to rush home and take me back to the hospital emergency room. It was the afterbirth left inside of me. The doctor removed the remainder without anesthesia or pain medication. What a miserable, painful experience. After I returned home, June-June and I started our bonding process. He was satisfied with eating, sleeping, and being changed. He was not a spoiled baby, always wanting to be held.

Chapter 9

Separation

EVERYDAY MESHA WOULD ASK TO hold her June-June. She loved him so much. I would allow her to hold him in my presence. A few days later, I left him in the bed and left her in the room with him. When I returned, June-June was not there. I asked Mesha if she knew where her brother had gone. She said "No." I looked throughout the house, calling to a baby only a few weeks old. She walked beside me, calling him also. Finally, she went into the living room and told me that he was there. She had placed him in the fireplace. We talked about it. I told her neither her June-June nor she should ever be placed in the fireplace. She said, "Okay mommy."

Life was really different now with two children. I was a very happy mother. June-June was my Mother's Day gift that year. I took Mesha to preschool and June-June to my maternal grandmother's house. She lived very close to the school where I was working. Seatbelt and car seat laws were not as effective back then. I would nurse June-June on the way to my grandmother's house and go to her house at lunch time. MoMo would always tell me what a good baby he was.

The four of us celebrated Thanksgiving together and were very happy. But by the time June-June was seven months old, James and I had separated again. I've always liked nice, small cars and wanted a new one. James Sr. wanted a big car. I gave in. We bought a 1979 Coupe de Ville cream-yellow Cadillac that was deducted from my check every month at the credit union. He told me to drive the car to work, and he would use it on the weekends. Our other car was a Volkswagen. James Sr. kept them clean, oil checked, and gassed up every week.

After we ate our Thanksgiving dinner together at home, the two children and I went to my grandmother's house to eat. We often ate at MoMo's house. James Sr. would never accompany us. I took pictures of James Jr.'s first Thanksgiving with a big drumstick. He was walking around in the baby walker. I tried to see if he would walk alone, but he did not. I remember giving Mesha her first drumstick, and she promptly took off walking by herself, taking giant steps. I took lots of pictures.

The day after Thanksgiving I did my Christmas shopping. I always get up early in the morning to go shopping. December 24, 1978, my late uncle, a very prominent minister in Baton Rouge, was on his way to California to be with all of us for Christmas. We always had a good time praying together, eating together, and being merry. I was excited. I got my two children dressed and ready to go to Mo-Mo's house.

However, to my surprise, James Sr. told me the car was not leaving the house that day. Being twenty-six years old, grown, working everyday, a mother of two children, I just knew he had to be kidding. I wondered, *Who is he talking to? Where are these jokes coming from?* As I attempted to walk out of the door, he grabbed Mesha and pushed her in a bedroom, then he grabbed June-June and threw him across the room, and finally he grabbed my hair, threw me on the floor, and beat my head as if it were a basketball. Again, I was physically abused. This time, June-June and I were taken to Kaiser Hospital. James had broken my thumb and given me a concussion. Fighting him was an impossibility. My two babies were hysterical. I still left with my children, but I was beaten up. It was Christmas time; it's the happiest time of the year for me. I had purchased the children toys and other family members gifts. I ended up being escorted by the Compton police to my home (that my great-great-aunt helped me buy for a wedding gift) to get my Christmas gifts. While I gathered the gifts, James called me many derogatory names. I am so grateful that the domestic laws have changed for the better and are now really being enforced. At that time, I felt like I was not being properly protected.

My parents were furious over this incident. I was forced to allow this cowardly man who beat me to remain in my home, because it was in both of our names. My children did not deserve to experience this kind of abuse. My babies were innocent. Why were they experiencing this? The children and I stayed with my mother and my late stepfather. I pretended to be happy, especially for June-June. It was his first Christmas. We had Christmas dinner at my late Grandmother's house with the entire family. I had a bruised face and my head felt like it was a large thumping ball.

I knew I needed my own space and independence. I felt crushed. My mother and stepdad did not mind us living there. My daughter attended school where my mother taught, and my grandmother kept June-June. I got restraining orders placed on James, and I stated that I was not ever going back to him. Soon, I left Mesha with my mom and stepdad. June-June stayed with my grandmother, and I lived in the Mustang Motel on Western Avenue.

James Jr. was such a good baby. My grandmother said instead of him crawling to where he wanted to go, he would roll there. If put in one place, he would stay right there until told to do something different. I missed being present to observe all of these precious little moments. I was very uncomfortable and did not feel right. I prayed that God would help me find a place for my children and me to be together under the same roof. I was a woman of faith then and still am. Jesus said in the Bible, *"And all things whatsoever ye shall ask in prayer, believing, ye shall receive"* (Matthew 21:22). I prayed, I believed, I had faith, and I received a new home for my children and me on May 25, 1979. My friend, Dorothy, who was in real estate helped me find the home. It belonged to a couple divorcing, who wanted out of the house. It had three bedrooms and two bathrooms. I thought it was perfect. And it *was* perfect. They wanted a large sum of money down and for me to assume the loan. Praise God for my church and my mother. I knew that being a faithful tither, I could go to my Father's storehouse. (Believe me, readers, the biblical principle of tithing works.) I went to my church leaders and my mother. From both of them, I got an interest-free loan. ***What a mighty God I serve***.

The three of us moved into our home and were very happy. My children did not deserve to be in a parental-abusive situation. God reminds me in His Word that He will supply my needs according to His riches in glory. And my children and I needed a home. James Jr. was one year old. We had no furniture, but praise God, we had a roof over our heads. That Memorial Day weekend, we went out and purchased a stove, refrigerator, and a bed for June-June and Mesha. We bought groceries; everything felt good. Thank God for Jesus. My pastor come over to bless our home. All I could say was what Jesus once said, *"Father, I thank thee that thou hast heard me"* (John 11:41).

Jr. was still in diapers. We had a brown dog, a boxer, named 'Mike.' June-June loved Mike. As a matter of fact, he loved all animals. He would go out in the big backyard with the dog. Mike would pull his diaper off, then June-June would bite the dog. They had fun together. We had a live-in nanny, who kept June-June very nice and clean. She changed his clothes at least three times a day and kept the house immaculate. She stayed with us from Sunday night to Friday evenings. The kids and I ate out every Friday night. In the summer, we did little things like picnic in the backyard. I had the outside of the house painted that summer, and we went to the movies and the beach during that time.

Because I was so embarrassed that my co-workers knew of my marital difficulties, I put in for a transfer and changed schools. It's called survival. I started working in Canoga Park, when I discovered June-June had chronic asthma and a lot of allergies. For a long time he did not talk. Doctors told me he would be retarded. When he cried, his mouth twisted, from dead nerve cells, the doctors stated. He just pointed at everything he wanted because he would not or could not talk. I took him to many doctors. Then I heard about acupuncture. I took him for that treatment, too. Now he talks. Thank you, God, for two healthy children.

Chapter 10

June-June's Life and Illnesses

I TOOK JUNE–JUNE TO the doctor for years, at least three times a week, to get shots for allergies and difficulty in breathing. Doctors told me he had chronic bronchitis, then asthma. He became terrified of doctors, white coats, nurses, and needles. I was at the hospital almost every night in order for him to use the breathing machine. The medication he received made him very sleepy. We were forced to get rid of his boxer because Jr. was allergic to all animals that had hair. We also had to remove the carpet from the house. I prayed a great deal as I gave him his medication.

By the age of two, his breathing had still not cleared up, and he sneezed quite a bit. June-June had a bad asthma attack while I was working in Canoga Park. He was taken to the hospital before I arrived. I nervously raced down the 405 Freeway to get to him, that was truly a nightmare. Whenever he had asthma attacks, I watched him breathe as though each breath were the last one. I transferred to a middle school in South Central Los Angeles during this time. By working at this school, I felt better because I was much closer to Jr.

One day when June-June was sitting quietly in the living room, or so I thought, suddenly all the lights turned off, and we heard a big boom. My son had stuck some keys into an electrical plug. The electrical shock turned his lips blue. He scared me other times, too. He would jump from his high chair to other chairs. I knew I had an active boy. I was happy about him, but anxious over his safety.

A few years later he wanted to follow my brother, his Uncle Adrian, who was going jogging, but riding a bike to the site. June-June rode on the back of the bike. However, on the return trip to the house, June-June's foot got stuck in the bike spokes, and he was badly hurt. A stranger, whom I consider an angel, gave him a ride to Mo-Mo's house. He cried nonstop. My grandmother applied some old home remedies to his foot, but the pain and tears persisted. His foot became infected. I took him to Kaiser Bellflower's emergency room, and the doctor immediately admitted him to the hospital. His foot was almost gangrenous. The nurse could not find a vein in his arm. He had roving veins. He screamed constantly. The medical personnel had to sedate him to put the I.V. in his arm. Each time they changed the I.V., he yelled. June-June remained in the hospital for six weeks. I worked during the day, and stayed with him every night. I felt so bad for him. His fear of hospitals increased.

I dropped June-June and his brother, Michael, at my aunt's house every morning before I went to work.

Her son and my two sons attended the same school. One day, June-June was in the bathroom, playing with matches. He set the toilet tissue on fire and tried to put it out with his hand. He burned his thumb very badly, and it became infected. He had second-degree burns. My aunt whipped him and sent him to school. The school called me about his burn. I was appalled and unaware of the accident. I left immediately. The burn was so bad, I could see his bone. The school authorities suspected child abuse and questioned both of us. I was very upset that I was not told about the accident until the school called.

One year while June-June was attending Audbon Junior High School, his head broke out in big boils. I took him to the doctor, who gave him medication. It was really ugly looking, but not contagious. The school erroneously thought he had ringworm. The kids teased him, and he got upset about that. The doctor gave him permission to wear a scarf and a cap until it got better. I was so upset the day he came home and told me his teacher joked about his head. People can be so cruel at times. My whole church, Academy Cathedral, prayed for him and in less than two weeks, his head had cleared up. Thank God that the prayers of the righteous availeth much.

Once, June-June and one of his associates fought on Crenshaw Blvd. The other fellow hit June-June over his eye with a crowbar. Blood was everywhere. The paramedics took him to the hospital, but he refused stitches and anything to do with needles. The doctor ended up giving him Tylenol and sending him home.

On another occasion in May 2002, June-June was driving someone's car on Freeway 105 and had a blowout, hitting his head badly. A lady found him wandering around the neighborhood and brought him to my gate around 3 A.M., asking if I knew him. I brought him inside, called his sister, Mesha, and brother, Mike. June-June refused to go to the hospital, so we called the hospital, who informed us that for a head injury, the injured person should not go to sleep. Keeping him awake was almost an almost impossible task. He loved to get his sleep.

June-June's Christian Life

June-June attended church every Sunday when he was a baby, toddler, and a teenager. He did not miss too much when he was a young man. He accepted Christ at a very young age and was baptized at a church on Florence Ave without me knowing it. I was kind of disappointed that I was not present at the baptism, but I was happy he had joined a church and accepted Christ as his personal Savior. He attended Sunday school and Bible studies. I was the youth supervisor at one of the churches.

June-June participated in the children's programs and made speeches during them. He spoke very well. As he got older, he would participate in church 'shut-ins.' When he started working in his last year of high school, he began tithing and did so faithfully until he departed this life. He served as a deacon and also served communion. He testified faithfully.

When Jr. was invited to birthday parties, it was so hilarious to watch him, because if he moved his feet, it would not be with the music, or if he moved his hands and arms, he would not move his feet. Oddly, he actually thought he was dancing. No one ever told him otherwise to make him feel bad. When prizes were given out, he still got one.

June-June had a special anointing. He could not dance as a young child to R&B music. He would dance as if he had two left feet, but he could really dance in the Spirit.

When he got older and attended Philander Smith College, he attended church there. He would call me and tell me I should have been present to hear the good message. I felt like my living was not in vain, having such a godly son.

Jr. often came to church, bringing his friends in his '95 Honda Wagon, which had a door that did not open. I laughed, watching as they climbed out of the window, trying to get to church. Like any normal young man, Jr. enjoyed music. Often I would hear him playing gospel and religious music. It did my heart good to hear him 'bumping' that kind of music. One of his favorites was Kirk Franklin's "That's the Reason why I Sing."

June-June's Employment

June-June started working at an early age. I am the previous owner of "Classie Fashions by Marie." I put on numerous fashions shows, and he and his brother did a lot of modeling of clothes for the shows. They modeled sports, casual, and dress wear. They recognized that there was real good money in modeling.

During June-June's last year in high school, one of my co-workers and dear friend, Robert Alcutt, hired my son in the youth program in Inglewood. He worked, diligently and faithfully. He did so well and never missed a day. Later, the city of Inglewood hired him to work at another location when the first job ended.

June-June also worked at Disneyland, in Fantasy Land. I was so proud of him. Grinning, he would get in the Honda that I had given him and drive to work. He had such a pleasant personality.

When he attended school in Little Rock, Arkansas, he worked for a pizza place. He also worked at Taco Bell, in Inglewood. His last few years of life, he worked construction and worked as an extra in movies. Two of those movies were *Little Richard* and *Coyote Ugly*.

June-June's Struggles on the Street

June-June struggled so much in life. He struggled with peer pressure, schools, mom, dad, gangs, and drugs. He did very well in his schooling. He was the school's student body president. He gave many speeches in school programs. I took him out of a private elementary school on West Blvd because a teacher slapped his little brother, Mike, in the face. Although June-June liked his school, that behavior was unacceptable, so I removed both of my sons from the school.

June-June's first encounter with the police was when he was only sixteen. He was driving back from work one evening and was late getting home, which was unusual. Mike looked outside and said, "Ma, the police have Jr. at the corner." I took off running down the street. One of the officers told me, "Miss, you cannot interfere with police business." I merely wanted to know what happened. Their response was that he looked only twelve, so he had to be giving false information to them because he said that he was born 5-6-78. I informed the police that that was, indeed, his birthday, and that he was not twelve. They let him go after checking his license.

Once, June-June went to McDonald's at Crenshaw/Imperial and gave the lady a $10 bill. She claimed it was a fake. He called me. I advised him to call the police for his own protection. He did. When the police arrived, the officer cursed him and told him he was gonna whip his a—and go home and tell his momma. Can we sometimes turn good young men into bad ones?

Another time I was working and came home one day for lunch. While I was in the bathroom, a van full of policemen rang my intercom and told me they would wait outside of my gate. They stated that my neighbors had reported drug activity going on in my home between 9:30 P.M.–12:00 A.M. I told them I had no idea what they were talking about, because I taught school during the day and worked for a major airlines from 8:30 P.M.–1:50 A.M. June–June was not home at that moment. The police stayed. Upon his arrival, they promptly arrested him and carted him off to jail. I had to hire an attorney to get him out. Later, he was found not guilty.

Once, Mike had a car accident. I woke June-June up to go and get his brother and have the car towed home with my AAA Card. It was not that simple.

When June–June arrived at the scene, someone was fighting his brother. He jumped in it. They called me. I called 911. Because *they* protected themselves, they were arrested. One taken to jail, and the other one sent to juvenile. Again, I had to hire lawyers and get them out of jail. They had been arrested for assault with deadly weapons (their hands). My sons had never had fighting lessons or karate lessons, yet their hands were considered deadly weapons. No one else was arrested. June-June had been sprayed with tear gas and had been cut, but interestingly, no one witnessed any of that at all.

Once during my fourth marriage, my baby girl, Elease, her dad, and I started out one evening driving his Rolls Royce to Santa Barbara. He had just bought the car. About the time we got to a service station, Mike called me and said, "Ma, the house is filled with police." We immediately returned home and found six police cars, one k-9 dog, and two police motorcycles there. I was so upset to see this. I just knew there must have been a murder. I questioned the police, who informed me there was a 'fugitive' in my house. I told them to let me go in and check out the situation.

Mike had told me the police started harassing both the boys at the liquor store on 110th and Crenshaw. They ran in two different directions. Mike was on a bike. June-June arrived home, and Mike said the police officer hit him riding the bike. He then ran. June-June opened our electric gate and let his brother in. I called the watch commander on duty at the police station. I will never forget how he came out and made them all disband. They had made a mistaken identity.

June-June had taken pictures of the police and talked a lot of crap to them before they left. After it was over, I told both of my sons to leave and go stay elsewhere for a few days. Mike did, but June-June told me he was not about to leave me alone when people play crazy games like that.

The very next day, June-June rode his bike with his friend to Winchell's on 108th and Crenshaw. Two of the police officers that had been humiliated were there. They arrested him for riding his bike on the sidewalk. A young man came and informed me of the incident. I ran down the street. The officers told me James was over 21, and if I did not move, they were going to arrest me for interfering with police business. I told June-June I was going home to make some calls. I immediately called the watch commander, again. He could not talk to me right then and hung up. Later that afternoon, I found out they were beating my June–June. Anyway, June-June was then sent to the hospital. I took both of my sons to Kaiser Lakeview Hospital, where they both were treated and reports were written.

After this happened July 21, 2001, I wrote Sergeant Aguirree III, thanking him for the professionalism in handling the incident at my home and the ticket given to June-June for riding the bike on the sidewalk. On July 27, 2001, my son received a letter about the ticket. It had been rejected by the city of Inglewood, and he did not need to appear in court. One year later, on July 26, 2002, my beloved son was murdered in the same neighborhood.

June-June and Sports

Jr. was ready for sports; he told me so. He had done a summer basketball camp. He wanted to play football. I enrolled him and his brother at a local park in Los Angeles. They played flag football, basketball. His coach liked him. Sometimes he would pick June-June up for practice and bring him home. On each team June-June played on, I volunteered to be the team mother. I prepared the snacks for each game. It was so much fun watching my sons playing sports.

I recall the first goal he shot in the basket, his first flag touchdown, and most of all, his first home run. Oh, the joy I had watching him doing something he enjoyed. Whenever possible, I videoed all of his games. When he entered his junior high school, a.k.a. middle school now, I changed him to a local park in Inglewood, where he actually played football. The first time my June-June was tackled, I remember running onto the field and being stopped by the coach, who reassured me that he was okay. That was all a part of the game. I just could not understand about tackling. But June really enjoyed the game, so I went along with it, too. June-June would often tell me he was going to make me proud of him. I always told him I was already proud of him.

When I first enrolled my sons in football, the funniest, most embarrassing thing happened to me as a single parent. The coach gave me a list of items that I needed to buy for them. I understood everything except one item—the cup. I called the coach and asked him was this a plastic cup, a Styrofoam cup, or what? The coach laughed and told me to go to a sporting goods store, and they would tell me exactly what I needed to purchase. Once I found out what it was, I was so humiliated and felt so ignorant!

When June-June reached high school, all he wanted to do was play football and baseball. I was a nervous mom at the time of the games. I could not understand the hard tackles he endured. He would always tell me he was all right. One Friday night, it was raining so hard, I told him I was not going to make the game. He came home later, as muddy as could be, and told me what a great game it was. I could not believe that he found it fun.

During those school years, I went to his practices so I could understand the game. I met a gentleman out at the practice once, and we talked. Both of our sons were named James. His family and I became close and started carpooling for the games, taking turns every week to drive. It was actually a lot of fun. The coaches urged me to stop cooking so much good food because the boys really looked forward to my good, hot, home-cooked meal every Friday, instead of looking forward to winning the game.

Once when I was still married to James, he went to see the boys play baseball at the Jackie Robinson Park. One of the boys lost his game, so James vented his anger by whipping Mesha. **Why?** To this day, I still do not know. I don't think Mesha knows, either.

June-June later attended a basketball camp in Santa Monica. He excelled in that. Mike received the Most Valuable Player (MVP) award. I was so proud of him, too.

June-June in College

June-June applied to go to many schools. He was accepted to LeMoyne-Owens, Philander Smith, and Fisk University. Because his sister was already attending Philander, he chose that school. Mesha felt like they could look out for each other there. Mesha was made queen at the school, and he escorted her to the ball. Soon he met a young lady, and the next thing I knew at Mesha's graduation, I was going to be a grandmother.

June-June's girlfriend called me collect from Arkansas while she was in labor. I stayed on the telephone until the baby, Jaylin, was born, December 8, 1996. I sent June-June first class on Delta Airlines to Arkansas to see his baby. He told me he was not well received while there. He was not even offered a meal. He had to sleep in a chair with a blanket. I told him to come home. It was Christmas time, and he did not need to be treated that way. I spoke to the young lady. She informed me that she was not going to feed anyone if she was not married to him. I asked if others visited, would they have to marry her before she fed them. June-June was really too young for all this madness. He had just turned eighteen when his baby was born. I did what I could do to help, but what is enough? I love my grandson. June-June never married Jaylin's mother.

June-June's Marriage

Years later, June-June met a lady who really captured his heart. He was so in love with her, he 'forgot' to ask me for my blessing on his marriage. Instead, he borrowed money from my mother and went to Las Vegas with the girl. He told us that his fiancée adamantly stated that she would not have any more children without being married and informed him that she was pregnant. So they got married January 2000. **However, it wasn't until August 5, 2001, that my granddaughter, Sydney, was born.** I was present at her birth. When the baby was born, her mother said "Oh no, the three of you all look alike," (meaning my son, granddaughter, and me).

He loved his wife so much and demanded that we respect her. He expressed this to me many times. June-June and I use to take trips together; he would call his wife and pretend he was somewhere else with someone else. I would be listening to him. He did anything to get love and attention from her.

One of the owner's of Gin's Liquor Store told me how much June-June loved his wife, and that my son would do anything for her. I agreed. She was the one that needed to know this.

When his wife was in labor, he wanted all of us there. Both of June-June's sisters were present, 'Chief, the Man,' (the father of my youngest daughter, Elease) was there, and I was there. June-June stayed at the hospital during the entire labor and delivery. I brought my daughter-in-law a beautiful gown to wear home, as well as some nice clothes for my grandbaby's home coming, and I brought June-June the video camera to take pictures. When I arrived at the hospital, I could feel a chill, a real coldness, in the room. I didn't stay. Later, June-June walked home crying. His wife refused to allow him to ride home in the car with her and his daughter. I told him he should have called me, but his integrity, pride and his manhood would not allow him to do so. I love my beautiful granddaughter, Sydney LeLani.

Prior to June-June's death in July 2002, he was very sad because I made him move from Inglewood since his wife had put restraining orders on him, and at the same time, had started divorce proceedings. He advised me to warn his brother, Mike, not to follow him in the streets anymore because he felt that Michael could not handle the streets. June-June went to live with his dad, but he still visited me everyday.

Chapter 11

Final Separation

JAMES SR. AND I STARTED seeing each other once again in 1980. What a glut for punishment I was. Not only did I allow my abusive husband back into my life again, I allowed him to move into my home in 1981. After he had done that, he fired my nanny, who had been taking care of the house and young June-June. Now I had to find another person to care for the children.

I found a baby-sitter on 109th Street, right around the corner from our home. She kept Mesha until it was time for her to go to school, and she looked after June-June all day. She told me June-June was a very good boy. Mesha was very protective of her brother, making sure he was fed when the baby-sitter cared for him and checking to see if he needed to use the bathroom.

James Sr. did not like the idea of the children being at a baby-sitter's home, so he found a day care to place them in. Both of the children were well cared for at the day care. The owners were very nice and later became very dear friends of mine. At this time, Jr. was four years old. I got him a little tuxedo and convinced him to ride on his maternal grandmother's Cadillac in the day care's King/Queen Contest. He looked so cute.

Much to my amazement, baby number three (Michael) was on the way. The children were delighted and both wanted a sibling just like him/her. I could not believe the age difference between the children. Each child was exactly four years apart. This truly was God's plan, not mine. And then ... domestic problems started again. **What am I going to do now?**

Nothing I did could satisfy my husband. I heard complaint after complaint. I got off work at 3 P.M. He expected me home no later than 3:45. If I arrived late, there was conflict in the form of verbal and physical abuse. I confided in my principal that I was experiencing domestic violence. At that time, I was the school journalism teacher and was expected to produce the school's newspaper. I also had church responsibilities.

The doctor placed me on work restriction due to pregnancy complications. He advised me to take early maternity leave. I was prohibited from lifting, vacuuming, mopping, extreme reaching, and anything strenuous. This infuriated my husband; he claimed all I wanted was attention. He warned me that if I were home everyday, the house had better be clean. I did what I could, but, of course, it was not good enough. We argued. I prayed and asked the Lord to help me. I knew that in the past, my church had helped me, my mother had also assisted me, and most of all, God had never forsaken me. So I prayed harder. I read the Psalms, I was like David in the Bible—I had to encourage myself. I would constantly quote, *"Weeping may endure for a night, but joy cometh in the morning"* (Psalm 30:5). I prayed, "Lord, help me get out of this just one more time." It was not healthy for the children to experience the arguments and the ensuing violence. Nor was it healthy for me and my unborn child.

When I was eight months pregnant, my husband tried to kick me, but I jumped out of the way just in time. Mesha was sitting by the bedroom door, crying, when the altercation occurred. June-June was probably somewhere in the house, in his own little four-year-old world. This happened the month of December. Well, the next month, June-June got what he wanted, a baby brother—he named him, Michael.

The baby was only two weeks old when I knew I had had enough abuse from this one man. God did not intend for a woman to be abused. James refused to be present in the labor and delivery room with me. He was present for the birth of our first two children, but not this baby. In contrast to his behavior, the infant's siblings were at the hospital, waiting for their new little brother. Michael stopped breathing in the delivery room. I was very afraid. Red lights were flashing, and nurses and doctors were rushing around, and my baby was pale in color. When he started breathing again, the doctors placed him in neonatal for several days. The naval cord had been wrapped around his neck.

The night before our discharge, the hospital provided a nice, candlelight dinner for the new parents. Well, I enjoyed a delicious filet mignon, baked potato, green beans with almonds, a tossed green salad, a piece of cheesecake, and a bottle of white zinfandel, but James refused to join me. My aunt came on standby. I sadly ate dinner with her, but the hurt festered in my heart. I knew I had taken enough abuse from this man. Neither did he arrive to bring us home. Praise God for a healthy baby, despite all I had gone through before his birth. God is a good God.

When little Mike was only two weeks old, I called my principal, requesting permission to return to work. But he refused, saying it was much too early. But I knew God would supply my needs because He said He would do it. I did not want my babies being a part of domestic violence any more, so I went to my ob/gyn and explained my situation. He okayed me to return to work, but warned me to be very cautious and call him if I felt ill. I prayed, asking God to let me escape from this man safely, with my three children, and I would not ever look back again. I was desperate. I needed divine intervention. I asked God to order my steps. The Scriptures say, *"The steps of a good man are ordered by the Lord"* (Psalms 37:23).

It was wrong for my children to see their mother abused. I became afraid of my husband. Early one Sunday morning around 3 A.M., I arose, wrote my husband an eleven-page letter and placed it under a pillow on the living room sofa, covered it with an Aretha Franklin album, then threw as many of my children's clothes in a large trash bag and stashed them in the car trunk.

I fixed breakfast as usual, dressed the kids, and left for the 8:00 A.M. church service. We stayed and attended both services, and then went to my grandmother's house. She and my aunt agreed to us staying there until we could safely move back into our home. Then I called my husband about 9 P.M. and told him to look under the pillow and read the letter.

I felt safe with my family members, but I was still afraid, so I got restraining orders and orders for the children and me to return to our home. The judge gave James three months to find a place to live, granted me full custody of the children, although James had visitation rights. I prayed that the Lord would help me raise the children correctly. The Bible says, *"Trust in God and lean not to my own understanding."* Thank you, God, for three healthy children. I give you all the praise, honor, and glory.

James was supposed to have the children every other weekend and every other major holiday. But he didn't always do that. Nor did he pay child support as he was ordered to. The courts had to garnish $125 per child from his check every month. One weekend, I brought the children over to him, but James came out with a gun, threatening me. I quickly left with the kids. Obviously, he did not want the children that weekend. As a matter of fact, most of the time, he did not want the children.

Eventually I transferred to a traditional school that had summer vacations because the middle school I was teaching at turned into a year around school. Now that I was a single parent and my children attended traditional schools, I needed to be with them as much as I could. June-June was about to enter first grade. I wanted to be there for him.

It was my first year teaching at the high school I graduated from (my dream was accomplished). I remember rushing home to get to my babies. June-June and his sister stayed at the day care across the street from their elementary school, and my baby stayed right next door with a very nice lady and gentleman, who used to take him to church three times a week and to a convalescent home to pray for the sick. Juggling my schedule, teaching, and caring for my children was not easy, but by the Grace of God, I managed.

After school was over, and if there were activities I needed to supervise (i.e., football, baseball, and school dances), I would rush home, bathe my children, and bring them with me. The next school year I was promoted to being a high school counselor. This was different, and better, than being a classroom teacher. By then, my baby was old enough to go to the day care also.

During this time, James came up to my church, Academy Cathedral, stating he wanted Mesha. I informed him she was in college. Then he declared that he wanted the boys. After I explained that they were on the evening program at church, he pulled a gun on me. I was unable to get anyone's attention, and no one at church was aware of what was happening. I reported him to the security afterwards and was given a whistle, in case it should ever happen again.

Chapter 12

Lil Girl Growing up with Nana Ella

MY NANA ELLA WAS MY great-great-aunt. From her, I got my prayer life. She listened to Mahalia Jackson songs, went to bed at 6 P.M. and rose at 6 A.M. Nana Ella lived until she was 99-years-old and died December 1974. She cooked with no salt and made her own butter. Every morning I threw breakfast away at her house because the butter smelled like stinky feet. Anyway, I survived the smells and appreciated her teaching me the way of the Lord. The two of us had prayer meetings every Wednesday night—singing songs and praying.

I was born in New Orleans in the Charity hospital and taken directly to her house after birth. She and her husband were married for 51 years, then he passed away. They had no children. My mother took me to Baton Rouge after she and I were strong enough to travel home, but every summer, I went to stay with my Nana Ella.

She bought my first piano, and she also put the down payment on my first home. After divorcing my husband, James, he received half of the sale of the house, plus seven years of my retirement funds because he had the audacity to claim that he helped educate me.

Nana Ella always told me that she had prearranged her entire funeral arrangements and she had willed me all her possessions. She did not believe in bills. "Pay everything in cash," she would always say. The Bible states, *"Owe no man debt,"* a rule she lived by. She owned a house in New Orleans, many acres of land in Opelousas, and a duplex in Opelousas. She had a large bank account, minks and furs. All I had to do was bury her. Her motto was not to let anyone take anything from me, because she felt like they were all fools. And she did not want me to be a fool, either.

After her passing, I inherited only $500, a cedar chest, and armoire; nothing more. I could not believe it. Certain relatives of mine had altered property into their names before her passing. I was too young to understand what had happened, but I knew it was not right. At that time, I was 22-years-old.

When I was in my 30s, my children and I flew to New Orleans and hired an attorney to find out the facts; however, the statue of limitations was over. I was hurt by my relatives' behavior. Why did they do this to me? But, I have forgiven them all in my heart. I have asked God to keep me humble in all things.

Even when I was growing up, I heard how relatives could be so greedy and vindictive. When their loved one dies, they mourn, they scream, they holler, some are quiet. But soon after the home going services are over, the greed kicks in and they change. I have had many experiences in that area.

December 24, 1974, great-great-aunt, Nana Ella, died and left me many nice things, money, property, minks, furs, diamonds, and furniture. She had paid for her own funeral services and burial. She had picked out and purchased her burial clothes. All I was supposed to have done was to bury her the way she desired, according to her plans. Well, that did not happen. Before I arrived at her home for the funeral, all her minks, furs, and diamonds had disappeared. She always had cash hidden under her mattress. There was not any to be found. The funeral services were at the Little Zion MBC, in Opelousas, Louisiana. I knew I was young, but I was old enough to know that things were not right. I had no say over anything. Why? Because I was trying to be obedient and listened to my older relatives, whom I trusted. Some of them just did what they wanted to do. I felt bad inside because I did not carry out my great-great-aunt's last wishes. I was told I had to appoint an executor since I was not living in the state of Louisiana. I was told who to choose. It was my uncle. For some reason, that did not feel right. When the attorney, my aunts, and my uncles finished with me, I felt like I had been raped. Of course, being 22-years-old, I did not really understand what was happening. No one in my family helped me. Everyone was too busy trying to see what was in it for them. They did get it all, except for $500. Later when I was older in my 30s, I could still hear my Nana Ella's voice saying, "Don't be a fool and let anyone take it from you. If they try, put them in jail." After thinking of those words, my children and I flew to New Orleans, Louisiana, and hired Attorney Peggy LeBlanc. She investigated and informed me of her discoveries:

Strangely, my great-great-aunt signed over her home in New Orleans to my aunt for a mere $2,000 cash. Her sister (my other aunt) was the notary, and their best friends living in California were the witnesses. These were my mother's sisters and brother. I could not believe that it happened. My late uncle then sold my great-great-aunt's two duplexes to a woman that became his wife. Now he's deceased, and she's the owner. It's baffling to me. What happened to all of my great-great-aunt's funds since she had no outstanding bills? From her entire estate, I received only $500 in cash. My own very close relatives stole from me.

Chapter 13

Stress and Death

ON FEBRUARY 23, 1978, MY PATERNAL GRANDMOTHER passed away. She was ill and did not want the family in California to know it. I had an odd feeling about her. She always would send me a fruitcake for Christmas and a birthday card with money on my birthday. Christmas came and nothing arrived, not even a telephone call. I could not locate her. My birthday came and no card arrived. I called her day and night, but got no answer. I knew she did 'day work,' better known as housekeeping, but certainly not all day and all night. I called my daddy. He just talked, but never did he tell me Ma Bessie was ill. I started calling hospitals. There were only a few in 1978. I called each one of them and asked if they had a patient called Bessie Milo and found her in intensive care. I asked the nurse to please put the telephone to her ear and let me talk to her. I was calling long distance from California. I was her granddaughter. I needed to talk to her. It was February 22, 1978. I told her I loved her very much, and I missed her. To my amazement, she was short of breath, but she told me she loved me, too. She told me to take care of my little girl and to take care of myself. We hung up.

The same day, James and I had an argument over me going to see my grandmother. He said "No." During the course of the argument, he kicked the telephone off the receiver and dared me to put it back on. Mesha's fourth birthday was the very next day, and I had planned a birthday party for her at her school.

Early on the 24th of February, my mother came to my house and said she had been trying to call me all night and that the line was busy. She tried to have the operator place an emergency call to release the line, but the operator told her the telephone was off the receiver.

My mother also said my Aunt Sweetie from Baton Rouge was trying to call me to tell me Ma Bessie had passed. I started crying, I was so sad. James showed no remorse. My mother advised me to go on with Mesha's party, which I did. When I got home, I asked James if he would go with me to my grandmother's funeral, but he refused. My younger brother and I flew to Baton Rouge. Mesha stayed with my mother. I was six months pregnant with my June-June at that time.

When we arrived in Baton Rouge, my brother and I stayed at my stepmother's house. He stayed in the same room with me and slept in a chair. He was watching over me.

My daddy told me I was not to do or say anything about the funeral. My Aunt Sweetie and Ma Bessie were very close. I was to let Aunt Sweetie handle everything. She did a beautiful job. Ma Bessie's sisters and cousins came from San Francisco, and they were hurt and sad because they did not know she was so ill. But it was Ma Bessie's wishes not to bother any relatives with her illness. My grandmother was so neat and clean. All her things just had to be labeled and boxed. Of course, there were relatives picking up items and talking about what they wanted. My Aunt Sweetie specifically stated what my grandmother's wishes were. She had a will. People do what they want to do, but there was no fighting or arguing—just stealing.

In August 1986, death hit again. *Oh, my God, I thought, that precious woman who kept our maternal family together was gone.* She provided us with true unity. All major holidays, we ate as a family and Mo-Mo led the prayer. She kept her children, kept her grandchildren, and she kept the great-grandchildren. I did an article about her in the *Sentential* newspaper. What a great woman she was, a sharecropper, and after the life and early death of my grandfather, Pa-Pa, she never remarried. She raised all five of her children alone with Jesus. All of her children went to college. Mo-Mo washed and ironed for all of us. She treated each one of us special. She was a very good woman, but when she said something she meant it. She spoke her mind. Mo-Mo moved to California in 1969. She was a good Christian woman that truly loved her family.

After spending many wonderful years with Mo-Mo, she started telling us about a severe pain she had in her side. I remember praying for her healing once, just the two of us. Shortly after that, Mo-Mo was admitted to the St. Francis Hospital, in Lynwood, California, and diagnosed with advanced pancreatic cancer. She passed away, and it was like, *'Wow, the ROOT is gone.'* There was a dinner at Christmas again, but it was not the same. To my relief, I won an all-expenses paid trip to Hawaii and was on the beach December 25th, so I did not have to remain in the area dealing with my grief concerning Mo-Mo.

Later, my mother and aunts decided they would open a school and church together. My children, my oldest brother's children, my aunt's son, and others attended the school. There was so much love and cohesiveness among us. But, there was nothing to fill the void that we felt from our loss.

More stress came in 1988. My daughter was attending Westchester High School. While she was leaving the dressing area in the PE room, the door closure fell on top of her head. She ended up getting her hair cut out and stitches put in. She was placed on home schooling and while this drama was unfolding, my oldest brother, Sululah Jr., became ill. He was such a beautiful person with a pleasant personality. He was ill and hid it. On February 8th, someone called the school office and informed me that my brother was very ill and had been hospitalized in intensive care at Martin Luther King Hospital. The assistant principal had someone drive me to the hospital. I could not believe my eyes. I loved him so much. He was the green-eyed monster with whom I always got in trouble. We loved each other. We had chicken pox together. We sold peanuts, competing to see who could sell the most. (Our dad used to porch peanuts since he was 13-years-old and still does. He is now 82-years-old.) We competed to see who could make the better grades, who could play the most musical instruments. He really got me when he was in the Marines. He took me to a concert and introduced me to one of his band member friends. He told me he had sold my clarinet to this guy. How could I get angry? He had so much charisma. Unfortunately, his wife left him with their three daughters at the time of his illness and returned to her hometown in New Jersey. It was not my business to ask why. I did know she needed to be aware of how sick my brother was.

We called her father and told him if she called, please have her call us immediately because her husband was in intensive care. She did call us, but refused to come back. Well, on February 13, 1989, Sululah Jr. passed away. My younger brother, Adrian, grabbed him and just cried. My daddy came from Baton Rouge. We all were so sad. My brother's death was so sudden, so unexpected. When daddy arrived at my home, he called his wife and had her send for my sister-in-law and my three nieces to come to be at my brother's funeral. My oldest niece cried the entire funeral. After the services, the children never came back to Southern California again. My momma helped my sister-in-law and the children when they lived in California. She was working at the school, and the children attended the school. My dad sent for them so they could be at their father's home going services. They have yet to acknowledge my parents with love, letters, or a simple telephone call. After my older brother passed away, Adrian was lost. He started going downhill. Once he came to my job and pulled a gun on me, demanding money. I ran into my friend, Alcutt's, office and screamed, "Lord, help me."

Then on January 13, 1995, my uncle, Huey died. His birthday was January 6th; he passed away seven days later. This uncle was a prominent minister in Baton Rouge, Louisiana. My mother could not attend the funeral because my stepfather was in and out of the hospital with a weak heart and strokes. Neither of my two aunts could attend either. Nieces and nephews came from all over. He had cousins and numerous pastors attend his home-going service. They held his service at the convention center. At that time, the family from the West Coast asked me to speak at the service. After the services, my younger brother went through some real drama with people on his back since all our first cousins felt they deserved a portion of the inheritance. My brother took care of this uncle in the last few years of his life.

Then, just three months later on April 2, 1995, my stepfather passed away in Daniel Freeman Hospital. He had had many strokes and his heart just gave out. He was a very good daddy to me. I loved him very much. He and my mother were a perfect couple. They used to go to church together, go fishing together; we all played cards together and ate together. He loved barbequing. I did not think he and momma knew each other's name. He called her "Baby," and she called him "Honey." One day I even asked them if they knew each other's real name.

When they got married, my stepfather had three

children of his own, and momma had the three of us. We were the Brady Bunch. All of us were close in age. We got alone as well as could be; daddy and momma did not let us get in their way. They helped each one of us as parents who care would. When daddy passed away, my stepsister and I were at his bedside. We gave him his last communion, then he passed away.

After his death, an ugly drama started at church. His children wanted to know what he left for them. Only one of them did not. They actually hired a paralegal to investigate. All they had to do was hear his last will. The officiating minister offered to read the will after the service, but they refused. He had left perfect, clear-cut instructions.

Then came 2002, and the death of my darling baby June-June. Oh my God, the deaths of all my dear, sweet, loved ones hurt, but Lord, when my son was shot three times to death, this seemed like all I could take. In my wildest imagination, I never ever dreamed of burying any of my children. I was numb, vulnerable, and broken. I found that people are out to get you when your guard is down. Not strangers—but very close relatives. There were so many people. My son knew everybody, it seemed. My ex-husband (James Sr.) talked to me. He said that whatever had happened to us in the past, that we should just put it behind us. **Yea, right!** When we got to the mortuary, he wanted to go as cheap as possible and even buy a feminine casket. He asked the counselor how anyone could tell the difference. I flew off the deep end. My daughter-in-law was there. She was also offended. I informed the counselor that I wanted the best for my baby. He lived a classy life, and I wanted him to leave classy. Because of my stern feelings about the burial of my son, James Sr. gave absolutely no money at all toward the funeral. He got a limo for himself, his mother, sisters, and brother. He did not put anything toward the family flowers. But he ***did*** collect on a life insurance policy on my son. Lillie, my friend, always says to me, "God sits high, and he looks low. He does not slumber nor sleep." I will make my last payment on the service we held for June-June January 2005.

His mother came to the city for the first time in her life, and not once did she call me. However, I did get a message through her son that she wanted to say a few words at the service. She greeted me from the pulpit with a "Hello to my sister in Christ." There was tension from the women drama. Also present was my first grandson's mother from Arkansas and my estranged daughter-in-law. Lots of drama! My grandson, Jaylin's, mother was constantly introducing herself as 'June-June's girlfriend.' My estranged daughter-in-law was angry and had nothing nice to say about June-June. Mesha was freaking out because she wanted to style her brother's hair for the service. She had done this many times for mortuaries, but we didn't allow it and tried to explain to her that this time was different. This was her brother and because of the gunshot wound to the head, it would not be a nice scene for her. She screamed and cried how she and her brother had discussed their last wishes. I did not want a dysfunctional daughter, as well as a deceased son, so I had to say no to her. Michael just stayed real quite and was very attentive to me and his little sister, Elease. Elease would cry out how much she was gonna miss her June-June. My newlywed Christian elder husband was too busy trying to let everyone know he was my husband at that time. He did not put one penny toward anything either.

The day of the service, I thought my baby was put away so beautifully. My friend 'Pa,' the late Bishop Ralph Artiaga, officiated. So many people came to honor June-June. A young lady gave me the $20 that she had received from him the day he was murdered. I still have it, thank you.

I want to express my thanks, again, to the pastor who allowed us to use the neighborhood church to eulogize James. It allowed so many of his friends and acquaintances to just walk to the service.

We had the repast at MG's (our church). It was wonderful. So many wonderful people, including family and friends, were there. Thank you Burroughs family for catering. You were excellent. Thanks, EJ, for my personal limo and the limo for my extended family. As I sat in the church and talked to people and friends I had not seen in a long time, my newlywed husband kept calling me, reminding me that we were newlyweds, and told me to come sit in the limo with him. **Was that sick or what?** I ignored those cell phone calls. You would think he would have shown some compassion during that horrible time. The straw that really broke the camel's back occurred when we were at the Inglewood Cemetery. He actually told me my grieving should end the day of the service.

Then, to top it all off, my younger brother had a good time talking negative about me from A-Z to all my ex-students, my nieces and nephews, my younger son, and friends. It all got back to me. There was no logic to it at all.

Chapter 14

Marriages Not Ordained by God

"What therefore God hath joined together, let no man put asunder" (Matthew 19:6).

OFTEN PEOPLE PUT THEMSELVES TOGETHER in marriage, not God. If my marriage to James had been ordained of God, nothing in this world could have broken it up. Through this union, God gave us three beautiful children. Shortly after birth and their medical checkup, the first place my children went to was church. The Bible says to *"Train up a child in the way he should go and when he is old, he will never depart from it" (Proverbs 22:6).* I took that advice to heart and took the children to the church, Bible studies, and Sunday school.

I remarried in 1984 (and divorced a year later) to a man who persistently chased after me. He had problems with my children. He did not accept us as a package deal. I probably forced him into marriage because I wouldn't commit to him outside of marriage. The responsibility for all of us was not on his mind. He was not physically abusive, but he was unfaithful.

In 1986, I was briefly married to my third husband, who was younger than I. This was a very short-lived marriage, just a meaningless fling.

I met my fourth husband at his job. My daughter was in his class. Mike actually had a physical fight with him in front of our door at home. My son told him that he was not going to pimp his momma. (Mike was right; he had more insight than I did at the time.) We got married, and God blessed us with a darling, beautiful little girl, Elease. But this man was also unfaithful. I caught him cheating so many times.

My fifth marriage was short, but not so sweet. This was a man of the cloth, but don't let that fool you. I chose an insecure, jealous, stingy, and demanding man to marry. He sits in church, praising God, shouting, and dancing. But he never brought one dime to the table, paid any of our bills, or bought groceries, and the list goes on.

I still wonder why I married him. He was mean to my friends when they came to console me during my bereavement from the loss of my son. He told me my grieving should have ended when we left the cemetery, as if I could turn my grief off at his will. He also made the selfish statement that he would have to learn to love my baby girl. As if that weren't enough, he was always calling his second wife and trying to make arrangements to be with his first wife and daughters. I have given up on my choices of husbands. God, I am waiting on You.

When I met all of these men, I was independent, working, had my own home, and was quite self-sufficient. I believe I have reaped what I sowed. I had the desire to be a happily married woman and chose my own husbands, instead of letting God do it for me. Now, I am dependent on the Lord and am confining myself to Him.

Chapter 15

Violent Attack

MY DAUGHTER AND I HAD GONE to the teacher's credit union in Torrance, California, on August 31, 1988. In route to my mother's house, a Caucasian man confronted us and flipped the bird at my fourteen-year-old daughter. She returned the gesture in kind. Driving down the street with the windows open, I stopped at the light. The man got out of his car, approached my car, then spit in and punched my daughter in her face. I took a bicycle chain from the car and began hitting him. He kicked me like crazy. Everyone around us was white. No one tried to help us at first. Then the Torrance police arrived. The police called it road rage, but didn't press any charges against the man. Mesha's nose was swollen; I had blood all over me, and my leg was incredibly swollen with a hematoma. We ended up at the emergency room of the local hospital.

I was placed on disability for the injury. I suffered both mentally and physically. The school year 1988–89, I was on sick leave, healing under the doctor's supervision. Mesha and I applied for assistance from

Victims of Violent Crimes and received less than $500 jointly. Then, on February 13, 1989, my older brother, Jr., passed away in the hospital. All this was almost too much for me to handle.

Chapter 15

Deep Throat

DURING THE YEAR I WAS on sick leave because of my disability. To my great distress, someone began calling the school, the area office and the superintendent, stating that I was, in fact, working at my mother's school while I was supposed to be on disability, that I was out socializing, and that I had transferred my daughter's grades from a previous school to her present cumulative school record. The latter was correct because I was a licensed, certified school counselor. I was simply unaware that it was not permissible to do this for a family member. I had worked years for the school system, being there at 6:30 A.M., sacrificing my free time to be involved in many miscellaneous, after-school activities, juggling my schedule to be with my children and do the school activities—now I became the bad person and all the good things I had done and accomplished vanished like smoke.

This nightmare dragged on for five years. Many depositions were taken, undercover cops investigated me, so-called friends deceived me, and others divorced themselves from me out of fear. These people were my friends, people I had loaned money to, ate meals with, carpooled with—and some of them were lying about me and testifying against me. **Why?** I was a single, working mother, paying my bills, caring for my children, and providing for their needs. I was happy with my job. Then suddenly, the devil tried to steal the joy and blessings that God had given to me.

I had a praying momma who stuck by my side through thick and thin. She helped me spiritually, mentally, and financially. I was truly a ball of nerves. The school board sent me downtown to do clerical work in an office until after the trial which had been initiated. I was stressed to the max. Different co-workers would come by and secretly warn me to be careful. I just did not understand what they were talking about. I knew I had been following the doctor's orders.

My case went to court. The opposing attorney gave stipends to some of my family members, co-workers, and so-call friends to come in and testify against me. No one was allowed in court but the mediating committee, the judge, the two attorneys, and whoever was scheduled to give a testimony.

The court went on for seven days. During that time, I had to listen to my family and so-called friends fabricate lies about me. One co-worker lied so much, the judge threw her out of the courtroom. On the fourth day, it was brought out that the person that had been calling the school and the area office complaining about me was given the name 'Deep Throat.' It was a woman who refused to identify herself. During the trial, the Los Angeles Unified School District

Attorney reported to the court that deep throat was my aunt and that she feared for her life.

Each morning before I went into the courtroom, my attorney, mother, and I prayed. Each day seemed worse than the last. But God was in control of the situation and took me through the dark tunnel with the sun shining at the end.

Seven is the number of perfection in the Bible. Finally it was over. I just had to wait for the verdict. My mother was with me everyday. She could not come in, but she was right outside. To my shock, I found out who Deep Throat was—my aunt—my mother's sister. My mouth fell open. I could not believe this. I had idolized her. I loved her so much. She lived with us in our home in Baton Rouge, Louisiana. I grew up with her. That really hurt so bad. Until this day, I still ask why she did it. It is beyond my comprehension.

Some people erroneously thought this case was only about money; it was not. It was my career. I could have lost my credentials that I had worked so hard for. My children and I could have ended up homeless. At a point in this five-year period, my children and I were on welfare, something that I had never been on in my life. One day in the mail, I received the verdict—not guilty.

By then, I was very paranoid. I did not know who to trust. In court, I found out that one of the assistant principals had his sister-in-law go to my family's school/day care and pretend she had a child to register. What she was really doing was trying to find out whether or not I was there working. It was stated in her deposition. The school had hired an undercover school police officer to follow me for thirty days, spying on me. People called my home, pretending to be other people, to see if I was there. In those days, caller ID did not exist. After listening to all this, no wonder I was so paranoid when I left the courtroom. It got to the point that I did not want to leave my house, I did not want to talk to anyone, and I would not let anyone in my home. At that time, I was dating a school police officer. Who knows, he might have been the undercover cop. Not only did I not want to socialize with people, I did not want my children to do so either.

Not surprising, I ended up going to a psychologist because I was a total mess. Thank God for an understanding, kind, and patient doctor. He put me on a lot of medicine. I almost gave up, but God kept me. His grace and His mercy sustained me.

Chapter 17

The Pulpit

AFTER HAVING BEEN BROUGHT UP in church with a firm Christian foundation, I ended up in the pulpit. For many years I listened to many preachers preach and some teach. I was so blessed that God saved me, sanctified me, and made me holy. I taught, sang in the choir, was a Sunday school teacher, youth supervisor, spoke at women's programs, got some valuable pulpit experience in the '70s at my uncle's church, and was a doorkeeper (usher).

God placed a special anointing on me. I give Him all the praise and the honor. Later in the late '80s and early '90s, again, I was a doorkeeper and enjoyed it. I attended church everyday. Then in the '90s, I joined a Missionary Baptist church. The minister said something to all of us that really disturbed my spirit. He informed us that he was putting all members on probation that were not tithing. I thought to myself, *Didn't Jesus walk this earth to save and heal the sick? What makes this man think he has that type of power?* Although I was tithing, I left that church.

After that, I started attending church services where my family owned the building. This particular minister previously made a statement in front of my mother and my late stepfather, that he would remain at the location in my parent's building until ***they*** put him out. But the ***next*** Sunday when I went to the church service, the pastor came in, put a sign on the door with the church's ***new*** location, and told me to follow him there because they were moving. I looked at him and stayed in my seat. I heard a still voice speak to me, *"Be still, and know that I am God."* So, I stayed. That morning, just God and I had church. Soon, I started having church right in my garage in Inglewood, Ca. June-June, Michael, and I talked to their classmates and friends in the neighborhood, and many of them attended. We had good church services. Some played the drums and piano, we sang, everybody gave testimonies. I taught the Word. It wasn't too long before we outgrew the garage. My family allowed me to have services in the building. This became MG's Full Gospel Church. 'MG' are the initials for my late maternal grandmother (Martha Greene). God had it all in His plan. I baptized over 150 people in 'God's water,' i.e., the Pacific Ocean. Not only did I baptize, but I also performed weddings, funerals, did counseling, visited the sick, the shut–ins, etc.

During this time, I decided to further my education. I enrolled in a Ph.D. program in Pastoral Ministry in August 1999 and graduated after completing my dissertation in "Women Pastors in the Local Church." It has been a very challenging, but rewarding job—being a woman pastor. Thus far, I have successfully celebrated seven wonderful anniversary services with my co-workers in Christ. There has never been and never will be a dress code for the church. I believe what Jesus said, *"Come as you are."* My children were all members of MG's. I baptized Elease Marie, my youngest child. Our church family broke bread together each and every Sunday. We gave to the needy. We loved. We knew each other by name, and we could sit around and be the body of Christ together. I truly miss my congregation. I still love each and every one of them, my evangelist and minister friends.

Chapter 18

Golden Birthday Year 2002

JANUARY 31, 2002 WAS THE YEAR I TRULY desired to see. I turned 50—it was my Golden birthday anniversary. The previous year in October, I had received my Doctorate degree. I was on cloud nine. The year seemed so different. On New Year's Eve, only Elease and I were home. Mesha was at her home, recuperating from surgery. Michael was vacationing, and June-June was with his wife and his new daughter. At midnight, the telephone started ringing. "Happy New Year, Ma!" It was June-June. I called Mesha because I knew she was probably feeling sad in bed, because she had just had surgery. We greeted each other and wished each other New Year blessings. Elease and I had already prayed. Every year my children knew we would be in church, praying in the New Year, or at home, praying together. This year, I cooked greens, black-eyed peas, fried chicken, potato salad, and corn bread. Because not all of my children were at home, it felt strange, really empty.

This month, I celebrated my pastoral birthday anniversary. 2002 was a very special year. God had blessed me to serve as pastor for the previous seven years at MG's Full Gospel, and now, I was approaching my golden age. Each Sunday, we were blessed to have great speakers: Dr. Franklin Sellers, Pastor Paul Cruz and Minister Paulette Cruz, Elder Tony Bryant, Dr. Rosie Milligan, Elder Eddie Atkins, and the late Bishop and evangelist Ralph Artiaga. I was personally blessed to have received many congratulatory awards from 49th assembly person, 35th district Congress woman, LA Unified Superintendent, California Governor, 45th assembly woman, 47th assembly man, a Senator, and many others.

On the last Sunday in January, Dr. Milligan spoke on "Fear to Faith." And Elder Atkins related the story about his son's death. Elder Atkins had been an inspiration to all people. He shared how painful it was losing his son and how God had helped him to heal. It was so touching. That night, January 27, my two older children came up for prayer and rededicated their lives to the Lord. I remember the thrill of it all and praising God. This was the greatest day of my life—to see my son, daughter, and about four other young people rededicate themselves to the Lord.

On the next day, January 28, June-June said, "Ma, let's go for a long ride, just the two of us. I want to spend quality time with you." He dressed in his nice dark-blue suit and his black kango hat and off we drove, going toward San Diego. We stopped and had breakfast, looking at beautiful homes on the way. June-June said, "I'm riding with the ***doctor***. We laughed, and I told him he could be a doctor, lawyer, or anything he wanted to be. We went shopping and bought his baby her first goldfish and some clothes.

Later, we stopped, ate dinner together, and he wished me a "Happy Birthday."

When we arrived home, he could not wait to take his five-month-old baby her goldfish. He asked me if he could work for Milow's Child Care doing odd jobs, so that he would have money to send to his wife for his daughter, Sydney. Instead of paying him, he had me send the money to Sydney via certified mail. Sydney's mother did not accept the mail.

February arrived with Valentine's Day. June-June got me a card and a rose. I was so happy. This son of mine was a special angel. He could humor people and turn lemons into refreshing lemonade.

On February 2, 2002, the Gospel host of KJLH, Andre Russell, came to my church to commemorate my golden year. We had jumbo jump, games, barbeque, potato salad, greens, yams, fried chicken, Cajun rice, chicken sausage, cake, and sodas. We had so much fun and Christian fellowship together. June-June helped cut the ribs and some of his friends came to celebrate this wonderful and great occasion. When he left, he told me how proud of me he was.

March arrived. It was a nice, quiet month. June-June worked at his job and helped his sister at her beauty shop, where she worked in the evenings. He would shampoo hair and clean the floor. He would then come home and go through his routine—kiss my forehead, take a shower, then go and hang out for a couple of hours. I cautioned him, and he would say that I was worrying too much. "I am alright," he would say, "I am covered with the Blood of Jesus." Neither my mom nor I wanted him to stay in the neighborhood anymore, even though he grew up in it, because so many shootings occurred.

When my sons were growing up, they were taught boys and men did not cry. This particular month June-June started crying in front of us, but would not tell us what was bothering him. Certainly one thing that bothered him deeply was that he was denied access to his baby, Sydney. I reminded him to hold on because God had his back.

Easter was on the way. The two of us went shopping and got his daughter and his step-son an Easter basket. He felt happy. Easter Sunday, his wife, and lil Sidney came over and ate Easter dinner with us. I was happy. We all were happy. We took pictures and just relaxed.

April brought in beautiful sunshiny weather, and flowers bloomed. Then my brother had domestic problems. I determined I would not get involved. But, I ended up going to Louisiana to support him. June-June went too, so that 'nothing would happen to his ma.' We stayed at my brother's house.

My brother's court day arrived. He got upset, so June–June took him outside by the Mississippi River and talked to him. When they returned to the courtroom, my brother had a new attitude. June-June was a peacemaker. Then we flew home first-class and the flight crew was extra nice to 'Mr. Charmer.' He really was celebrating his 24th birthday.

When we arrived home, I planned our annual Mother's Day celebration. On May 10th, all the ladies in my family and ladies from the neighborhood came to my house. No men or children were allowed. We had nameplates for all the guests and enjoyed a delicious meal of King Crab legs, boiled shrimp, and lots of other mouth-watering delicacies.

Although no men were allowed, guess who showed up? 'Mr. Personality' (June-June) himself. He walked around the table and gave all the ladies a kiss and a promise of a $20 bill.

Shockingly, three days later, my sensitive, loving son was served with restraining orders from his wife and was forced to go to court.

In May, June-June appeared in court. He acted proper and never lost his composure. His mother- and father-in-law witnessed how he was very respectable, with excellent manners. They testified that they had never seen June-June hit or abuse their daughter. He handled his case very well under those difficult circumstances. I was very proud of him. His heart was very heavy.

On Memorial Day weekend, I got a call from Jaylin, June-June's first child. He asked me to come to his Pre-K graduation. I hesitated and told him I was going to send him something nice. But, he said, "Granny, *please.*" I told him okay. Then I informed June-June that we needed to make reservations to see his son graduate. June-June was really happy. We packed, bought tickets, and flew to Little Rock, Arkansas.

Jaylin's mother and grandparents were very happy to see us. Jaylin jumped in his daddy's arms like he was a little baby. They had talked on the telephone, but they had not seen each other since Jaylin was seventeen-months-old. What a delight it was to see my son and grandson reunite and start bonding. Jaylin is my first grandson and my college surprise from when his daddy was attending Philander Smith College.

We all went to dinner that night. June-June asked Jaylin's mother to forgive him for any hurt and pain that he had put her through. He told her he had made mistakes and to please forgive him.

The next day, we went to the graduation and videotaped and took pictures of the ceremony. That Friday night, Jaylin stayed at the hotel with June-June and me. He followed his daddy everywhere he went. They were both laughing and were so happy together. June-June took time to teach Jaylin how to swim.

Later, Jaylin's maternal grandparents came to get him. Jaylin really did not want to say good-bye to his dad. They hugged, kissed, and did a hi five. When he kissed me, his maternal grandmother let him say a Scripture to me. "Granny, *I can do all things through Christ Jesus who strengthens me.*" Oh my God, I was so elated. I hugged him and told him to call me collect whenever he felt like it. Then we flew back to California.

The month of June arrived. I told June-June to stay with his daddy and give me a break because I was not feeling good. I had headaches and chest pains. He did not want to leave me, but did. Yet, he would come every evening to see about me before he went home.

On Thursday, June 20, I became very ill. An ambulance rushed me to the hospital. As soon as my children found out, all of them came there. June-June looked at the heart monitor and said "You ought to stop faking; you're gonna be alright." I was hospitalized seven days.

Upon discharge, June-June wanted to stay with me, but I insisted he stay at his dad's house.

July 18, my mother called me and told me Mesha's godfather had passed away, and that his funeral services were being held July 26. On Sunday, July 21, I announced to the church that we would be having prayer meeting Tuesday night, Wednesday night, and Friday night until midnight. I had never announced prayer meetings three times a week in all of my seven years of pastoring. I often ask the Lord to order my steps and to keep me in His will. I felt this was His will, and I was obedient unto it. It was soooo strange.

July 19, I had a vision, or a dream. My mom called me and said a friend had called her, stating that her husband had passed away. In this vision or dream, I replied that we were preparing to bury one of our own family members, too. It was frightening. I told my mother, and she said, "Girl, don't say that." Though I didn't know it, my God was preparing me for **The Terrible Night**.

Chapter 19

The Terrible Night

JULY 26, 2002, I WAS BEING FAITHFUL and obedient to God, in His will, praying and asking Him to save my children, to cover them with His precious Blood, to be with them and protect them if I'm dead. I had just finished clapping my hands when the telephone rang. It was my neighbor, insisting I come home immediately because of an altercation involving James Jr.

My husband, the musician, Melease, and I immediately got up and started out the door. I called my next door neighbor. I wanted her husband to go and see what was going on. He did and reported that somebody had gotten shot but it was not June–June, according to him. The person shot was "KK." I said, "Lord, that's what the people call June–June in the neighborhood." My neighbor also told me that a lady had ridden her motorcycle to my house and was screaming for me. I drove home in my van, saying, "Oh God, this can not be true. Oh God, if Jr. is shot, let it be in his leg or his foot. Please, God, nothing serious." Before I arrived, my cellular telephone rang; it was my neighbor again, telling me that Jr. had been shot in the head. I shouted, "Help me, Lord Jesus. Oh my, Lord Jesus." I got weak in my body, and then I started shaking. My foot was trembling on the accelerator. I tried to call my daughter, but only got her voice mail. I tried to reach his dad, but only got his voice mail. I tried to reach my mother. All I got was her voice mail. I was able to reach my brother and told him Jr. had been shot in the head and that's all I knew. "Please pray like you never prayed before." My husband took over the driving. I told him to go to the beauty shop where my daughter did hair.

"Have you heard the news Mesha?"

"What, Momma?"

I screamed, "Jr. has been shot in the head, and they took him to a nearby trauma hospital."

"Why aren't you there, Momma? Go, Momma!"

I told her I could not get there. I was so nervous, scared, and shaky. I remember getting back in the van, feeling numb, but saying "God, don't fail me now. You are the same God I was praying to in the church. You are the same Lord that healed the sick and raised the dead. Do it for me, Lord!" I did not want to drive to Crenshaw Blvd., where the shooting occurred. I was crying, "The Blood of Jesus! Jesus! Jesus!" As we drove, it seem like it took us forever to get home. I did not even try to go to the hospital to see my child all shot up. I could not think of any enemies that Jr. had. He was well liked and loved by everyone.

When I got home, my niece called me, so I had her go to the hospital to see if it was true.

My telephone rang. It was my oldest daughter, telling me in a voice that I had never heard before, "Momma, June-June didn't make it. He died." I remember **screaming** at the top of my voice, "Oh no, no, no!" I fell on the floor, screaming, "No, not my baby." I threw the telephone down and cried. I ran out my side door and screamed for my neighbors. "Jr. is gone!" Oh no, this cannot be true. I cried and cried and cried! My five-year-old baby girl asked me, "What happened?" I told her, "Your June-June has been shot. We have no more June-June." She started crying. She got his senior high school graduation picture and cried until she had a headache. Then she finally went to sleep.

I called my momma. She already knew. Someone had called her. For some reason, momma's words were comforting. "Marie, you did everything you could for him in this world." We hung up. I called my daddy in Louisiana, and he said, "Oh Lord, have mercy." He could not handle it. He began to cry. He told me to call him the next day. It was already 9 P.M. here. It was 11 P.M. there. My neighbors started coming over immediately. They took my telephone book and started calling people to let them know my Jr. was deceased. My house had so many people saying, "I'm sorry." I could hear them, but I was feeling so numb. I hurt so badly. I was empty. I was in shock. I was like not living here on earth. It was like being in the twilight zone. Who could be so cruel to take someone's life with a gun and not think about the family? Mesha and Mike went to the hospital to identify June-June's body. *Oh my God, don't even ask me to go to a hospital and see my baby all shot up, and when he left home earlier today, just four hours ago, he was full of life. He was a happy person, and now he's dead.* He was so happy, full of life, and full of jokes. He gave me a bag of cookies and said "Here 'Grandma,' have some Grandma cookies." I told him to be careful and to stay out of Inglewood. He said, "I'm not afraid to die." That day, he asked me if I was going to go with him to his friend's funeral, who had just been shot, on Saturday. I responded, "No, Junior. I just left your sister's godfather's funeral today." He kissed me on the forehead, as usual, and said, "Ma, I'll be back."

He left his work clothes on the top of Mike's car. He took a shower, and that was the last time I saw my child alive. I don't understand why it happened. I was empty, numb, and basically, just dumbfounded. I don't have any answers. I believe in God. I know that *"All things work together for good to them who are called according to His Purpose."* I love God, and I know He makes no mistakes. I still hurt, so I've decided to write about my son James and our relationship from his birth to his death, in hopes that by retracing our beginning, it will help bring closure to our temporary ending.

I know I will see James again. I wrote of this agony in the end of my book because this was my last hurt, and it hurt more than all my other hurts. This pain was worse than all my other pains. These tears I shed were like no other tears. I find comfort in knowing that God promised to *"Wipe away all tears."* He said it, I believe it, and that settles it.

May you, the reader, find hope and comfort through my experience, if you have suffered such a loss.

Chapter 20

My Prayer for My Son

Prayer:
"Heavenly Father, the death of my dear son, James Russell Johnson Jr., has filled my eyes with tears and my heart with sorrow. I am distressed by the mysteries of Your providence. As Your humble child, I want so much to say, not my will, but Thine will be done. But at times, I find it difficult to do. Forgive me and help me, I pray, by your Holy Spirit, to accept Your ways as always best.

"Holy Spirit, apply to my wounded heart the healing touch of Your precious promises and let me soon experience their power. Teach me not to mourn as those who have no hope. Wipe away my tears, that I may be able to see through the mist beyond death and the grave to the resurrection and life assured by the glorious victory of my Savior Jesus Christ over death and the grave.

"May the passing of my son remind me that I, too, am but a pilgrim and a stranger on the earth. Grant me the grace to love less the things that are material and temporal and to love more and more the things that are spiritual and eternal. Teach me to number my days and apply my heart to the wisdom taught by Jesus Christ; He is the Way and Truth and the Life. No one comes to You but by Him. Speak through Your servant, Holy Spirit, in the precious name of Jesus. Thank You, God. Amen."

Chapter 21

Home Going Celebration– I Eulogized My Son

I GIVE HONOR TO THE Most High God, who truly is the head of my life. Also, to my brothers and sisters in the ministry, to James Sr., to my children, grandchildren, my mother and father, my ex-mother-in-law and father-in-law, all my relatives and friends. We are not here for sadness. We are here to celebrate James Jr.'s home going. James was a happy-go-lucky person. He would not want anyone crying today. He is gone to a better place.

It is not easy to eulogize your own son, but I was privileged to be James Jr.'s pastor for the past seven years. No one could know him better than God and me (his mother) for the past twenty-four years.

James entered this world May 6, 1978. He was a unique child. The doctors told his father and me that he was not going to talk. I can remember when he pointed to everything instead of talking. We prayed for him. How many of you know about the power of prayer? James had a very humorous personality. I reminded him of his pointing episode not so long ago; he told me, "Ma, I didn't have anything to say at that time."

When he was born, his older sister gave him the name 'June-June.' I have so many precious memories of James. After his first checkup with the doctor, his next stop was church. How many of you know the Bible says, *"If you train up a child in the way he should go, when he is old, he will not depart from it?"* James had an astute personality and was very intelligent. Always a hello and a smile. He did little things for people. It's really the little things that count. He was a caring, well-mannered, and respectful young man. James had a name for everyone. I will miss him saying, "What's up, fat lady?" His older sister was "Esha," his one and only brother was "Nigel," and his baby sister was "Little Bad Girl." When you saw James, you saw his younger brother, also.

He told us, "I'm going to make you proud of me." We kept telling him we were already proud of him, but he repeated, "You just don't know how proud I'm going to make you of me, Ma."

At the end of April this year, he traveled with me to Baton Rouge, Louisiana, to see my daddy, who talked to Jr. almost every day, telling him to follow the Bible and to live right. He bought Jr. a black suit. I kept asking him when he was going to wear his new black suit. He told me, "Ma, I've got my time to wear it; don't worry." He was with his uncles and aunts on both sides of the family and his paternal grandmother. He took pictures and had a good time.

James Jr. loved his son and daughter. In May, my grandson, Jaylin, graduated from pre-K in Little Rock, Arkansas. James got a chance to see him and taught him how to swim. Jay was so afraid of the water, but before we left the swimming pool, Jr. patiently took time to help him to overcome his fear of the water. June-June had a chance to see his son's mother and grandparents and they all had a very good time together.

June-June also loved his grandmame (his maternal grandmother). He would always give her a kiss on her cheek. That was her 'June Boy.'

The Bible says, *"Teach us to number our days"* and *"Be ye also ready"* (Matt 24:44). James was ready. Everyday James would leave work and stop to say, "What's up, fat lady?" as he checked to see if I was okay. He would say, "Hey" to his friends, catch the blue line, and go home. I would tell him, "Boy, you don't have to come to Inglewood—just go home." He said, "Ma, I know what I am doing—my life is in order."

On Friday, it was a little different. When we said our hello, he gave me a bag of Grandma Cookies. I said again, "Jr., stay out of Inglewood. As he left, he responded, "Ma, I'm not afraid to die." His favorite Scripture was, *"No weapon formed against me shall prosper"* (Isaiah 54:17). I was in our church praying. I had just finished saying, "Lord, save my children. Cover them with Your Blood,"—when the telephone rang with the news that my James had been shot. There is a message here.

"Children, obey your parents in the Lord for this is right" (Ephesians 6:1–3). Listen, these are words that parents throughout the universe are constantly say-

ing. Being a parent is not an easy role in this society. It's an awesome responsibility. I'm sure all of us parents have a story to tell. On this earth that the Lord God created, He, the Lord God, gave us instructions, laws, and commandments to follow. Sometimes as young people, we nod our heads and say we understand. But sometimes we just don't understand the meaning of a word. Let's break down the meanings: **Instructions** are imparting knowledge to others. **Laws** are an authoritative rule of conduct, and **commandments** are rules imposed by authority. What am I saying? If God gave us instructions, laws, and commandments as parents, we have to hear, listen, and obey. *"Children, obey your parents in the Lord for this is right. Honor thy father and mother, which is the first commandment with promise that it may be well with thee and thou mayest live long on the earth."*

First, let's talk about the role of parents. The father is the parent responsible for setting the pattern for the child's obedience in the family. Any discipline the mother does is and should be an extension of the father's authority in the home. Well, in 2002, about 68 percent of African-American homes only had one parent. Yet, we are told that the husband or the father must take leadership in this area of the family, and the wife and mother must be in submission. Genesis 3:14 reads, *"In sorrow thou shalt bring forth children and thy desire shall be to thy husband and he shall rule over thee."* That's the Word! You see, the father's responsibility is set forth in two ways: First, the father is not to provoke. "*Provoke not your children to wrath.*" God does not want us to abuse our children. Parents are not to overly discipline children or reign in terror with the result being that the child can only react in a blind outbreak of rage. Second, the father is to "*Bring them up in the nurture and admonition of the Lord.*" To 'bring them up' involves three ideas:

- *It is a continuous job*. As long as the child is a depen-dent, the father is to be responsible for providing for the child, in order that he becomes what God wants him to be.
- *It is a loving job*. To 'bring up' means to nourish tenderly; children should be objects of tender loving care.
- *It is a two-fold job*, involving nurturing a child's needs for his development—physically, mentally, and spiritually.

A child's disobedience is not to be tolerated. "*He that spareth his rod hateth his son; but he that loveth him chasteneth him betimes*" (Proverbs 13:24). How many of us are guilty of sparing the rod? We, as parents, have a responsibility to train up our child in the way he should go, and when he is old, he will not depart from it. Now the word says to you children, you young adults, **obey**, which means submit to the authority of your parents in the Lord. For it is right.

Children, listen to your mother and father, for it is right in the Lord. Either you are going to do right or wrong. God's way or the devil's way. If you chose to do it your way, get ready to experience some bumps, some bruises, some heartaches, and pain. This comes with disobedience. Disobedience is rebellion against recognized authority. There are two ways to do something: the right way and the wrong way. The Bible says, "*Obey your parents, for it is right in the Lord.*" Hallelujah, thank You, Jesus, for being a righteous God.

"*Honor thy father and mother.*" You are esteemed, or regarded highly above all when you obey your parents. This is the first promise. You know if mom or dad promises you something, you look for it. I tell my children all the time, "I am your mother, and I love you. I'm not going to do or say anything to hurt you; I want only to help you." The same with God. He loves us unconditionally.

James loved the Lord. He prayed. He attended church. He was a tither. He would help serve communion. Often he would say, "Ma, pray with me or pray for me." It was no accident my June-June's birthday was 5/6/78. He was special. It may seem hard that James is gone, but "*To be absent from the body is to be present with the Lord.*" Church, I am not super human, and I know that I have had to say over and over again, "Earth has no sorrow that heaven can not heal." Thank You, Jesus, for giving me strength. James touched the hearts of many. He is smiling now. Folks that have had broken relationships for years have come together today, and, James, it's because of you. Baby, I'm proud of you.

To our family and friends, June-June is free. His life was in order. James' life ended at age 24. He has no more worries down here. No more crying, no more disappointments, and most of all, nobody can hurt him now. For consolation, the Apostle Paul says, "*Eye hath not seen nor ear heard, neither have entered into the heart of man the things which God hath prepared for them that love Him.*"

Goodnight, June-June. I sure will miss you, Baby. I have so many precious memories that will always be cherished in my heart .

Chapter 22

Face It, It's for Real

AUGUST ARRIVED AND I COULD not cope with anything. I could not drive. I was unable to go anywhere but to church. And then, someone drove me there. I stayed home in unbelief. I was in denial. I did not want to believe June-June was gone. I waited everyday in my blue reclining chair between 3 and 3:30 P.M. for the doorbell to ring, waiting for my June-June to come through the gate and us go through our little daily routine.

Some days I would even get up during that 30-minute period and push the button to open the electrical gate. I was in true denial. My life seemed so dreadful. I felt useless. I felt numb. Friends would call and make statements, "You'll get over it. It's okay. Everything will be normal again." It really made me not want to talk to anyone. I was told to call an organization in Inglewood for mothers who lost children to violence. A nice lady there told me, "*I know exactly how you feel.*" I started to hang up on her, then I thought, *Let me talk this one out.* "No disrespect to you, Miss, but how many children have you buried?" She said none, but she had the experience of talking to other mothers who had. I told her there was no comparison between talking about and actually experiencing something. One acquaintance told me to let the dead bury the dead. *How could those words even come out of someone's mouth?*

On the 26th of August, my niece came and took me to the cemetery. Previously, I had religiously gone out to Inglewood Cemetery, where my grandmother (MoMo), my brother, (Jr.), and my stepfather (Isaac) were buried. I would take flowers and just sit out there sometimes. *My God*, I thought, *how on earth could I really be visiting my happy-go-lucky son's grave?* It was not an easy task. I cried and cried. I went back home and still waited for the doorbell to ring. Neither Mesha nor Michael would come over. They couldn't stomach the thought of coming back to the neighborhood, knowing what happened. They love Elease and me, but they wanted us to move to another part of California. Oh Jesus! I could not even get myself together to preach or teach. Every time I tried, I would cry. I asked my spouse, the Elder, to take over for me. He copped out. He told me he was an elder, not a pastor, and never wanted to be one. I tried to do what I could to hold church. My members were very understanding. They were right there with me. I was hurting so bad. The pain was indescribable. What topped it off, I had married an insecure, jealous, overbearing man, who had no idea or understanding of what I was experiencing. All he cared about was us being 'newlyweds.' I could not have cared at all about being newlyweds. I was crazy with grief.

One Sunday, Mesha decided to take me to brunch in Orange County. She picked me up from church. It was obvious I had not been eating. I left church during Sunday school. Openly, with no respect, my elder husband yelled across the church, "**Gloria, do not leave this building**." I looked at him. The Sunday school members looked at him. I did not say anything—I left. My husband told everyone present that Sunday school was over and ordered them to go home. He fired the musician, then locked the church gates. I went to the brunch at a quiet restaurant in Orange County. As I attempted to eat, the food seemed to grow larger than my mouth could bite or chew it. When I returned home, with Mesha, the musician called me to ask why he was fired. My husband was waiting to interrogate me. He asked why I disrespected him and disobeyed him. I told him to leave me alone and get out of my life because I could no longer deal with his selfishness, his insecurities, his jealously, and most of all, the lack of support he gave me. He informed me he was not going anywhere. He was my husband, and he demanded my respect. At that moment, Mesha spoke to him, "I think my mother asked you to leave. Please do, so we won't have to experience any problems. We are dealing with enough right now. Don't take us through anything else." He looked at me and left.

September arrived, and I called a psychiatrist that I was referred to. Evidently, this doctor must have been the greatest next to Jesus because he was booked in advance for three months, and then, the earliest he could see me was 9 P.M. I explained to him that I had not been capable of driving yet and needed a daytime appointment. I was paranoid. Of course, I did not get to see him. I kept crying out to God about how much I was hurting. Oh, it was a hurt that no one could feel but my God. He was the only one who could feel my pain. Oh, Lord, how it hurt. I finally got the nerve to drive one day and drove to a shopping center, where I locked my keys in the car and left my cell phone in the grocery store. I sat down and cried. I could not handle it. I saw a locksmith getting into his van in the parking lot. He opened the car door for me, and I paid him.

I decided to return to work at a school to keep me extra busy. One of my ex-fellow classmates was the principal of a school, and he hired me. That was a tremendous help to me. My daughter, Elease was attending the school. She was also hurting from the loss of her brother. She would express how much she missed him and just cry. She talked about how he used to take her skating, to the donut shop, and out on our street during Christmas to see Santa.

We would ride to school together, eat lunch together, and leave school together. This was good therapy for her. Elease is my little buddy that sticks by my side.

November arrived—my first holiday without my June-June. I didn't know what I was going to do. Mesha and Mike did not come over anymore. I only saw them on Sundays at church. In the past, we were all together. I usually cooked a turkey, ham, and brisket; vegetables; dressing (rice & cornbread); potato salad; about seven potato pies; and two cakes. I bought all the ingredients. This year I wanted to cook, but did not have the energy. I got up on Thanksgiving morning, then Elease and I rode bikes at the beach. We started out on our ride, and I heard a voice, "Ma, cook dinner like you always do; I'm still going to be there." I looked around, but saw no one besides Elease, so the two of us went home and cooked a nice turkey meal with dressing and all the trimmings. She and I blessed our food and had a great dinner.

Later, we visited my late Bishop, Ralph Artiaga, and his lovely wife. He was ill. We prayed, and we talked. I thanked him again for officiating June-June's home going service. Bishop told me he saw me having a giving-up spirit. He told me God would not be pleased with me. He told me he had gone in to his bishop and planned his own home going services. I did not want to hear this nor accept this. I started crying. He assured me it was definitely a better place. I tried to ignore him. I told him he had to open up my anniversary service in January 2003. Either he or Ma Me (his wife) had to do the opening and speak. He told me that he could not think of a better person than me to receive all of his pulpit furniture, the baptism pool, and all of his personal items for the pulpit. He and his wife walked me out to the garage and showed me what he wanted me to have. He gave me his blessings.

December was here, my favorite part of the year. I wondered how I would survive without my oldest three children. We were so use to celebrating together—eating, talking, videoing, and opening and exchanging gifts. My bishop passed away December

15th. *Oh my God! No!* I thought. *He knew what he was talking about.*

On Christmas Day, Elease and I spent a quiet Christmas. Her daddy decided not to be a part of her life for Christmas. (He did not even greet her with a 'Merry Christmas.') The mayor of Inglewood sent her a big sack of toys, KJLH Radio gave her a large bag of toys, and many artists and movie stars sent her gifts also. We had a Merry Christmas. My heart was still heavy with grief, though. I could not stand the house any longer. I heard a still voice telling me to move. I packed our clothes, we flew to Las Vegas, December 26th, then to Hawaii on the 28th. I could not even bear the thought of hearing gunshots on New Year's Eve. It made me sick to my stomach.

Hawaii was so beautiful. We saw all the fireworks from our hotel room. Elease was fascinated.

January 2003 arrived. I received a divine message—move to another state. The state was named. I kinda ignored that. I didn't know anyone there. Elease won the Martin Luther King contest for six-year-olds in the city of Inglewood. She appeared on TV and had about seventeen speaking engagements to present her speech. I was so proud of her. My birthday anniversary was celebrated at MG's as usual. I had lost so much weight. It was obvious that I was not eating—just grieving and hurting. I decided to give my home an uplift. I painted the inside and the outside. I got new carpet for the whole house.

I had begun a ministry on radio station KTYM called, "Stepping out on Faith." My theme music was

"Everything that happens to me that was good, God did it."

February arrived, and I was still very sad. I heard a voice again saying, "Get up and leave for ..." I started arguing with God, reciting all my accomplishments: I was the founder and pastor of MG's, I had a child care; I was working.... God stopped me. He said, "I know. I am the same God that gave all of it to you." So, I started calling moving companies for quotes, and I started packing like I was a crazy person, I moved and never looked back.

March arrived and I found a moving company and finalized all arrangements to move. I called my masseur. She came over, and I talked to her about it during my massage. My family did not want to believe me. Mesha told me I should move somewhere in California, but not to go to an extreme, like what I was planning.

By April, I had packed everything I owned. My family told me I could not run away and asked me what I was running from. They said, I should stay home and pray. But, I had heard from God Almighty. And that was the final word. I gave momma her birthday presents and a big vanilla, whipped-cream strawberry cake for her birthday. Elease and I flew to our new destination to look for a new home.

In May, on Memorial Day weekend, I moved out of the house I had purchased twenty-four years earlier in Inglewood, California. I found a location for our new home and watched the builders construct it from the ground up. I was a woman of faith. That same weekend, I found out from one of my girlfriends in California that a mutual friend had lost her son. Oh, God, was I sad for her.

By the end of June, Elease, Mike, and I had moved into our new home. We "stepped out on faith."

Chapter 23

Stepping Out in Faith

"NOW FAITH IS THE SUBSTANCE *of things hoped for and the evidence of things not seen*" (Hebrews 11:1). I often asked God to order my steps, and now I needed to put obedience into action. On Memorial weekend 2003, we temporarily moved into a three-bedroom condo until our home was built. We were so jammed-packed in the condo with all our boxes and furniture, we could not move. We had no space at all. We stayed in the condo for only one month, but it seemed like it was forever. Elease did not have space to play, and she could not be as vocal as she was used to being. I had to stay focused; I was on a mission.

By the end of June, we moved into our lovely five-bedroom home. We were so happy. We celebrated with a big barbeque the 4th of July.

Never will you hear me say or see me write that I didn't experience the devil. I have had my challenges right here. Starting with ministers, contractors, finding employment, principals, a very sad transition with my son, Mike, and dealing with everyday life situations—I have had attacks.

Even in the short time I've lived here in my new residence, I realize the devil doesn't leave you alone. He comes in like a flood. But as the song writer says it so clearly, "The Devil don't like it when you're blessed like that." I know that "... *no good thing will He withhold from those who walk uprightly*" (Psalm 84:11).

I take God at His Word. "*All things are possible to them who believe.*" Everyday for years, I have written on my calendar, "Praise God for this day." **God Loves Me**. Every night before I close my eyes, I thank God for everything that has happened the entire day. Believe me, I have gone through loneliness, and every time I tried to cry, I could hear the Lord's words, "*I'll never leave you nor forsake you.*" I've gone through and still continue to go through a different way of living. God has blessed me, and truly, I am so grateful. I am not the same.

In my present position, I mostly work with males. Ain't no play here. Been there, done that. I listen to statements like "I (a female) don't belong in that position." One thing I have to say—if I didn't belong there, I would not be there. I belong to God. I am a child of the King. He is an on time and a righteous God. I will be there until He moves me. I am like a tree planted by the waters, and I shall not be moved.

Chapter 24

Conclusion

I HAVE CARRIED ALL THIS hurt around for as long as I can remember. I thank God that He has allowed me to forgive myself and to ask His forgiveness. I must go on with my life in a positive and godly way.

In all my struggles, I've been blessed. We all have a story to tell or skeletons in our closet. I don't mind sharing my story because it was therapeutic for me. I strongly hope I can help some young lady or ladies that have been abused in the church or keep them from being abused. I also hope this helped heal a hurting mother who might have lost her child to a violent crime. And lastly, I fervently hope that my testimony can aid hurting women who have been physically or mentally abused by their spouses. The Scripture exhorts elderly women to teach the young women. I was ashamed before, but not anymore. I am not happy over what has happened, nor am I crying about my life. I only want to help the ladies that get caught up in this madness.

As Joel Osteen says, "It's a wrong thinking pattern that keeps us imprisoned in defeat." I had been programmed to so many negative thoughts by relatives, some ministers, some teachers, and some friends. "I would never make it." As you can see, those were lies. My time is now. I must forget about my past.

Everything I've gone through is over. My past can not and will not determine my future. God said that He would give me a *"twofold recompense for my former shame."* That means if I keep the right attitude, God will pay me back double for my trouble. God will add up all the injustices, all the hurts, and the pains that people have caused me.

I have worked from babysitting, cleaning houses, going to the auction selling cars, selling conservative ladies clothes, teaching, counseling, day care, airline work, and investing in houses. Those jobs paid off. Being a mistress and madam did not. Fast living does not.

My biggest dream is to meet and speak with all the hurting, abused women that have experienced this sort of thing in the church, regardless of the city, state, or country in which they live.

If you are interested in contacting me, please email me at: ClassieM@cs.com

Let the words of this song, "What a friend we have in Jesus" get into your spirit.

>"What a friend we have in Jesus
>All our sins and grief to bear,
>What a privilege to carry,
>Everything to God in prayer.
>Oh what peace we often forfeit,
>Oh what needless pain we bare,
>All because we do not carry everything to God in prayer."

Rev. Dr. Gloria M. Milow

Seventh Pastor's Anniversary

&

Golden Birthday Celebration

Seventh Pastor's Anniversary
&
Golden Birthday Celebration
for

Rev. Dr. Gloria M. Milow
Sunday, January 13, 2002

M. G.'s Full Gospel Church
6570 South Normandie Ave.
Los Angeles, California 90044
Elder John W. Wiley Co-Pastor

Message from Rev. Dr. Gloria M. Milow

Praise God from whom all Blessings Flow. Thank God for allowing me to stand in the stead of a pastor. I've experienced emotions of glee and there have even been times of sorrow. However, the glee has more than surpass the sorry. God never said the road would be easy.
I'm very thankful and very excited because I believe that on this 7th Anniversary of my pastoralship, God is aking me and us as a church to heights untol so I look forward to my continued service in this vinyard.

Respectfully & Prayfully,
Rev. Dr. Gloria M. Milow

Sunday, January 13, 2002
11:00 A.M.

Theme," *God's Courageous Woman*"

Opening Song	"This is the Day"
Escort the Honoree	Elder John Wiley (Everyone Please Stand)
Scripture	100 Psalms Elder John Wiley
Prayer	Elder John Wiley
Intro to M. C.	Elder John Wiley
M.C.	Sis Phamesha Johnson
Flowers	Sis Tamara & Leticia Nelson
Welcome	Sis Gloria Fontenot
Response	Visitor
Praisers	M.G's Choir
Tithes /Offering Announcements	Sis Phamesha Johnson
Tribute	(open to friends) 3minutes
Intro to Speaker	Sis Phamesha Johnson
Solo	

Guest Speaker	Dr. Donna Price
Invitation to Christ	Elder John Wiley
Acknowledgements	Sis Gloria Fontenot
Remarks	Rev. Dr. Gloria M. Milow
Song	"Happy Birthday"
Benediction	Elder John Wiley
Refreshments	

"O Taste and See that the Lord Is Good" Psalms 34:8

Sunday, January 13, 2002
3:00P.M.

Theme, "God's Courageous Woman"

Opening Song	"What a Mighty God"
Escort the Honoree	Elder John Wiley "Everyone please Stand"
Scripture	"34 Psalms"
Prayer	Elder John Wiley
Intro to M. C.	
M.C.	Sis Sophia Gillett
Flowers	Sis Tamara & Leticia Nelson
Welcome	Sis Kesha Nelson
Response	Visitor
Praisers	M. G's Choir
Announcements	Sis Sophia Gillett
Tithes/ Offering	
Tribute	Open to Friends (3minutes)
Selections	Eternal Word
Intro to Speaker	Sis Gloria Fontenot
Solo	Sis Lizzetta Patterson

Speaker	Rev. Dr. Franklin V. Sellers *(Eternal Word Church)*
Solo	Sis Lizzetta Patterson *(West Angeles COGIC)*
Invitation to Christ	Elder Wiley
Bless the Baby	Elder Wiley
Acknowledgements	Sis Sophia Gillett
Remarks	Rev. Dr. Gloria M. Milow
Benediction	Rev. Dr. Franklin Sellers
Refreshments	

The Lord is My Light and My Salvation whom shall I Fear?" Psalms 27:1

Thanks to My Heavenly Father and all Members, Guest and Friends. Words can not truly express how much I love each one of you and what a great day you have made it be.

God Bless You

GOVERNOR GRAY DAVIS

Commendation

Reverend Dr. Gloria Marie Milow

January 27, 2002

It is a great pleasure to recognize you as the M.G. Full Gospel Church honors your invaluable contributions at your Seventh Appreciation Services.

I applaud your commitment to providing spiritual guidance, moral leadership and service to the Inglewood community. Your efforts to build the personal and spiritual connections essential for social and religious life have made a lasting impact.

On behalf of the people of the State of California, I extend best wishes for continued success.

Gray Davis
Governor Gray Davis

STATE CAPITOL • SACRAMENTO, CALIFORNIA 95814 • (916) 445-2841

California State Assembly

Certificate Of Recognition

PRESENTED TO:

Rev. Dr. Gloria Marie Milow

M.G.'s Full Gospel Church

IN HONOR OF:

*Your Dedication, Outstanding Services
and Your Commitment to Provide Strong Leadership
to M.G.'s Full Gospel Church*

"Rev. Dr. Gloria Marie Milow's Seventh Appreciation Services"

January 27th, 2002

Judy Chu

MEMBER OF THE ASSEMBLY

49th ASSEMBLY DISTRICT
CALIFORNIA STATE LEGISLATURE

CERTIFICATE OF APPRECIATION

PRESENTED TO

Rev. Dr. Gloria Marie Milow
M. G.'s Full Gospel Church

IN RECOGNITION OF
YOUR OUTSTANDING SERVICE.

BARBARA BOXER
UNITED STATES SENATOR

January 24, 2002

Certificate of Appreciation

presented to

Dr. Gloria M. Milow

in recognition of her Seventh Appreciation Service and in appreciation of her dedication to M. G's Full Gospel Church and to the community

Maxine Waters
Member of Congress
35th District, California

On this 27th of January 2002

Maxine Waters
Member of Congress
35th District

California State Assembly

Certificate Of Recognition

PRESENTED TO:

Reverend/Dr.

Gloria Marie Milow

IN HONOR OF:

On behalf of the California State Legislature, I am honored to join with M.G.'s Full Gospel Church, in paying homage to you for your many outstanding deeds and years of exemplary service to the community

January 27, 2002

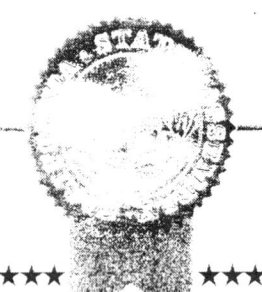

Herb J. Wesson Jr.
MEMBER OF THE ASSEMBLY
47th ASSEMBLY DISTRICT
CALIFORNIA STATE LEGISLATURE

James R. Johnson, Jr.

The Transition

IN LOVING MEMORY OF
James Russell Johnson, Jr.

ORDER OF SERVICE

REFLECTIONS

OBITUARY & TRIBUTES

Alpha: May 6, 1978 ~ Omega: July 26, 2002

In Living Memory Of
James Russell Johnson Jr.

May 6, 1978 - July 26, 2002

My Son was Murdered!!!

Rev. Dr. Gloria M. Milow's son James R. Johnson Jr. was killed July 26, 2002

Inglewood City Council Offers $50,000 Rewards

INGLEWOOD—Mayor Roosevelt Dorn and City Council members approved an amended initiative that offers $50,000 rewards to any individual or persons for information leading to the identification, apprehension and conviction of the person(s) responsible for the deaths of two Inglewood residents, James Johnson and Jason Allen Scott.

First District Councilman Curren Price recommended the initiative on Aug. 21, when the families of the two victims told their stories to the Council. While the Inglewood Police Department continues to investigate the incident, it is hoped that the offering of a monetary reward is an effective strategy towards apprehending, identifying and prosecuting the person(s) responsible for the crime.

Last month Johnson and Scott were fatally struck by an unknown person(s) firing a weapon in a parking lot of a business located on Crenshaw Boulevard.

For more information about the reward or the case, contact the Inglewood Police Department at (310) 412-5290.

$50,000 Reward
Wanted Information

JAMES R. JOHNSON, JR.

On Friday, July 26, 2002 at approximately 8:20 p.m. at Gin Liquor Store – 11001 S. Crenshaw Blvd., *James R. Johnson, Jr.* was gunned down. If you have any information regarding this homicide, please contact: Detective Burton at the Inglewood Police Department, Homicide Division (310) 412-5246. (All information will remain confidential).

$50,000 REWARD

WANTED INFORMATION

ON FRIDAY, JULY 26, 2002, AT APPROXIMATELY 8:20 P.M., AT GIN LIQUOR STORE 11001 S. CRENSHAW BLVD.

JAMES R. JOHNSON JR.

WAS GUNNED DOWN

IF YOU HAVE ANY INFORMATION REGARDING THIS HOMICIDE PLEASE CONTACT:

DETECTIVE BURTON AT THE INGLEWOOD POLICE DEPARTMENT, HOMICIDE DIVISION (310) 412-5246

(ALL INFORMATION WILL REMAIN CONFIDENTIAL)

BOOK AVAILABLE THROUGH
Milligan Books, Inc.

Secrets: Sin, Struggle, Stress, Surviving - $14.95

Order Form
Milligan Books, Inc.
1425 W. Manchester Ave., Suite C, Los Angeles, CA 90047
(323) 750-3592

Name_____ Date _____

Address _____

City_____ State____ Zip Code ____

Day Telephone _____

Evening Telephone _____

Book Title _____

Number of books ordered___ Total........... $ _____

Sales Taxes (CA Add 8.25%)..................... $ _____

Shipping & Handling $4.90 for one book . $ _____

Add $1.00 for each additional book .... $ _____

Total Amount Due .... $ _____

☐ Check ☐ Money Order ☐ Other Cards _____

☐ Visa   ☐ MasterCard Expiration Date _____

Credit Card No. _____

Driver License No. _____

Make check payable to Milligan Books, Inc.

_____   _____
Signature   Date